WALKING

&

WHEELING

TALES

Maureen T Corrigan

WALKING & WHEELING TALES

Maureen T Corrigan
Visit my website at www.maureentcorriganauthor.com.au

Printed in Australia

First Printing: December 2020

Shawline Publishing Group Pty Ltd
www.shawlinepublishing.com.au

Paperback ISBN- 9781922444325

Ebook ISBN- 9781922444332

Maureen T Corrigan

For many years, Dr Maureen Corrigan was a medical practitioner who worked in a broad range of healthcare roles, from general practitioner to hospital and health service CEO.

She retired early because of developing multiple sclerosis (MS). Maureen is now able to pursue her many other passions, including travel and writing, which has led her to say, 'I sometimes think getting MS was the best thing that happened to me!'

CONTENTS

Maureen T Corrigan

INTRODUCTION

I love travelling. Going to new places, growing in my mind and learning new things. It's exciting. Sometimes I think it's like an addiction and I have to do it. But I also want to do it and need to do it. It's part of keeping my body moving.

In 2006 my world changed when I had to retire early because of multiple sclerosis (MS). I'd had a successful career in the health industry and there was a lot more I wanted to achieve but had to leave. My body stopped working properly.

MS is an autoimmune disease where the myelin sheath surrounding nerves is attacked and destroyed in patches. That results in interruptions to the electrical signals directing bodily functions and movement. My mobility was the first thing to be affected. I bought the gear I needed as the need arose to help me keep moving and doing the things I loved.

Because I wasn't working, I had a lot more time. Managing a chronic illness takes time, but I also had spare time. With that I could do more of the things I loved doing such as travelling. I also discovered I enjoyed writing.

In 2016 my first book was published *Unexpected Rewards: Travelling to the Arctic with a Mobility Scooter*. It is about my first overseas trip with my new Luggie scooter and only one person to help, in 2011. The trip was such a success and gave me so much confidence, I just had to write a book about it.

Travels with my scooter since then have often ended up with many funny stories from things that happened along the way. I've ended up having more interesting and funny times than when I travelled without it.

I cannot travel alone as I did on my first trip overseas many years ago in 1976. I need Sue, my best friend and flatmate to help me these days. She travels with me everywhere. We are a great team.

Some of my travels in recent years have been back to countries I visited when I was much younger. Picking up my first travel diary–My Trip, gave me some insights into those times I'd forgotten. I read it again to see how my travelling ways might have changed and what I did so long ago. I have changed. But the same passion for travel is still there.

I've written seventeen travel tales here about some of my travels over forty-seven years. A few are when I was younger, others more recently with my scooter, decades later.

I hope you enjoy reading them.

In opening

A Woman Who Goes Out Walking/ A Local Travel Triptych (2020) Section 1

There is a woman who goes out walking on the pier once or twice a week. She's been doing it for years. Well, ever since the old pier became the new one, capable of being walked on again, in 2011. But in 2020 she was out more often and sometimes walked up and back on the pier twice. She looked straighter too, a neighbour said, less bent over, weaving her way around people, keeping her social distance during the COVID-19 pandemic.

On Princes Pier, Port Melbourne, the woman walks out confidently and keenly over the two hundred metres of smooth level concrete to the end where it meets the water and original pylons are left standing. The 'forest of piles' is an architectural feature extending south, a further three hundred and fifty metres into Port Phillip Bay.

In good light and no wind, the water turns into a mirror reflecting the pylons. Professional photographers take photos and bicycle riders, venturing off the bike trail, meet for a group photo. Travellers sometimes come to see them too. The place rates well on TripAdvisor. The woman stops and looks curiously at the shapes, textures, colours and reflections, wondering if she'll take another photo. Could it be better than the one she took the other day?

Fishermen are usually at that end of the pier over deeper water. They have more than one rod positioned waiting for a bite. The woman looks interestingly into some of the buckets to see if there is anything in them. An old man fishing one time held up the snapper he caught for a photo.

Heritage information stands on the pier tell its history—the use for ships and troops in World War II and later, passenger ships arriving with immigrants. Sometimes the woman stops and reads the stories again, in case she learns more.

Once or twice the woman has gone in a circle around the pale green, two-storey building in the middle of the pier. The heritage listed gatehouse was once used as a ticket office amongst other things to administer ports. The gatehouse has been restored and school children now use the upper floor for art classes.

The woman usually walks back on the right hand, western side of the pier through the open gates where a rock groyne nearby protects the shore.

Sometimes she sits on the high-backed wooden seating where the sun streams down, unobstructed by the tall buildings along the shoreline. In pre-COVID days she might look around and follow the seaplane landing over at Williamstown before moving on. But all international travel ceased in 2020, and there were no visitors coming to see the bay or coastal sights.

When she walks on, she passes over the old railway tracks, ground-down and left in the newly concreted pier. Trains used to run between the pier and the city, transporting wool, wheat or other goods. The old, rusted lines have been left to remember the story of the 'new railway pier', as they called it in 1915.

The woman goes around the modern rusted-look metal pergola at the start of the pier with multi-media screens inside that stopped working a while ago. She had enjoyed reading some of the personal stories of Greek and Italian migrants arriving over the years. She wonders when the screens in the heritage information kiosk will be fixed.

Her pier walk is then back to where she started, on the walkway and bike trail going around Port Phillip Bay.

Two hundred up, two hundred back with fifty across at the top and the bottom, makes a rectangle of five hundred metres. In the past, another two fifties across and back made her six hundred metres in twenty minutes benchmark. She has been doing that for years until these last few months when she is doing more.

If she does a second round of the pier, she walks more slowly but still in the same clockwise direction, starting on the east side of the pier. The woman might sit at the edge on one of the six commemorative bench seats made of old timber kept from the pier renovation. They have the names of old ships engraved on the front—such as SS *Nea Hellas* or SS *Wooster Victory*. The woman wonders about those ships and their story. She Googled the names later and discovered they arrived in Port Melbourne in February and May 1949. The names of passengers on the ships are listed and referred to as refugees and displaced persons migrating to Australia after World War II from various European countries.

Or the woman might look further east over the water to the nearby International Cruising Terminal at Station Pier. In the past she saw different cruise ships moored and recalled her time on board a ship overseas somewhere. But cruise ships were not docking anymore in early 2020, and she thought she had probably done enough cruising, anyway. Time to explore other means of travel again.

However, the Spirit of Tasmania is still docking daily at Station Pier, carrying goods going back and forth across Bass Strait. Campervans, caravans, cars and trikes used to form long lines waiting to get on the ship. But during the pandemic, Tasmanian borders were closed to visitors, and no one was holidaying there.

Sometimes there are dead sea creatures near the edges of her pier, starfish mostly, that look attractive but apparently are pests. The woman keeps a close eye on the water too for any sign of movement in case dolphins appear again or another small whale or sunfish.

She walks on again between the bench seats and a line of five large round concrete plantar boxes with trees planted up high, to reach the open metal gates. The historic gates are on both sides of the two-storey gatehouse and painted the same heritage light green colour. Pigeons sit chatting on that side of the gatehouse roof while seagulls fly around everywhere. It is a good half-way marker of one hundred metres along the pier. By then sometimes the woman looks like she is lost in her own world, just walking and thinking—solving a problem or trying to find the best word to use.

Those fishing are usually beyond the gates, nearly always male, and look like they have a mix of Asian ancestries. They might sit on one of the benches overlooking the pylons or a make-shift seat near the edge with their fishing boxes and buckets. The fishermen are on the pier all day in all sorts of weather. Some are on their own, others in small groups chatting or listening to the radio in another language. Sometimes they just sit there looking out to sea towards Antarctica or over the bay in deep contemplation. They seem to barely notice the woman walking past.

There were no fishermen out in the first months of the pandemic with lockdowns. Fishing was not part of the exemptions for the Stay-At-Home order. But the woman continued to walk out there and look at the forest of piles. Tiny fish still moved about with the occasional run of jellyfish. Seagulls sat on pylons and flocks of birds and swans still flew over.

She comes back on the west side of the pier again and looks over to Williamstown, the Westgate Bridge and Webb Dock at the mouth of the Yarra River, thinking about what might be in those shipping containers piled up high. Commercial ships continued to come and go much the same during the pandemic.

The woman walks on past the landing point on the pier with steps down at one end and a ramp at the other, all with shiny marine grade stainless steel railing. A few boats occasionally come into dock. But they are small and might be involved in maintaining the pier. In January, a larger boat is briefly there for the Greek Orthodox Church Blessing of the Waters ceremony. Young men board the boat, then after it moves away, dive off trying to be first to retrieve the cross thrown into the water. The woman likes to watch the event each year.

Cormorants dive into the water on both sides of the pier, but on the west side there is more competition near the beach when swimmers are out. The woman sometimes stops to look at one standing at the end of the rocky groyne.

Dog walkers often come towards the woman on that side, after their time on the beach when dogs are allowed to run off leash.

Another set of commemorative seats are at the pier edge with the names of more ships engraved. *SS Svalbard* is on one, and the woman pauses to look and think. She remembers the place she visited in the Arctic years ago and wonders why a ship has the same name, making a mental note to look that up sometime.

Sometimes she swings her walker around and sits on it, looking at though there is nothing wrong with her and hasn't a care in the world— like she does not need a walker. The concrete is so smooth her walker can turn around quickly. The pier is perfect for roller skaters, and sometimes people do figure dancing in the open areas. The woman doesn't look like she'd try doing that.

With the COVID-19 pandemic, no-one was sitting on the pier. People were out but everyone was moving, allowed out once for daily exercise, social distancing. Throughout the restrictions the woman kept moving too, continuing her walking exercise but not on the pier on weekends when more people were there. She wasn't out for very long, about thirty minutes in the past, but in recent times her walks could last forty to forty-five minutes.

Council COVID cleaners came on to the pier twice a day during the pandemic, spraying seats and cleaning surfaces that might be touched - tops of rubbish bins, handrails, signs, the tops of bollards and the like. They wore bright orange fluoro jackets and sun protection hats carrying spray bottles and cloths. Five or six of them moved efficiently around the pier cleaning, east to west, in a clockwise direction, the same as the woman.

In the past, the woman would occasionally sit on one of the seats at the start of the pier and stretch out her legs, putting them up onto her walker. But during the pandemic, she especially did not want to sit there so close to the bike trail. She thought there would be too many people whizzing past on bikes, some talking loudly and spraying the air or others jogging or walking past talking on their mobile phones, all producing aerosols. The airborne virus might be there too. After one round (five hundred metres) or two (one kilometre) the woman left the pier.

Princes Pier Port Melbourne

There is a woman who goes out walking most days around the neighbourhood's streets, parks and gardens. It's usually late morning, and she walks in different directions along the footpaths. Beacon Cove is a relatively new housing development where some might think the houses look the same, but the woman always finds something different. She looks around everywhere as she walks and occasionally stops to take photos.

The woman doesn't look old, but she's not young either. Her outfit matches, but it's not showy and always includes running shoes with low socks. Socks that are often black and pushed down but occasionally short white ones, like the Bonds ones from Coles.

Her pants are usually black but in summer they could be grey, shorter and baggier. In winter they're tighter. Though recently they seem to be tight ones all the time.

Most times the woman has some sort of hat on. She has a collection of them in different colours with narrow brims and most have something embroidered on them—*Australian Open*, *Davis Cup* or *Wilpena Pound Resort* to name some. But there is one beige hat with a broad brim more suitable to Australian hot sunny summers that she used to wear all the time. But not so much these days in Melbourne's different sunny Autumn.

In summer she usually wears a short-sleeved shirt of some bright colour over the black pants. In winter she wears a zip up orange or purple polar fleece jacket and a navy and white check scarf. Bright colours, but not necessarily fashionable.

There is a walking stick folded in half that sits in the walker basket beside the seat. She takes it out sometimes and uses it to help her walk away from the walker, to get closer to a flower, a plant or a cat in a window (a dog would bark and that had not turned out well in the past). The ground she walks over looks as if a walker would have great difficulty moving over it.

One time after she stepped closer to a flower to take a photo, the walker rolled off on its own with the walking stick in it. Each step she took to reach it was very slow and careful, gingerly lifting one leg at a time. She didn't fall, but you could see why she needed a walker.

When the roses are blooming, she often stops to smell them. Some are old garden heritage roses in front of original worker's cottages and two-storey 1880s terrace houses, sitting in strips near the newer houses. Sometimes she takes a photo of one close up, studying the layers of petals and colours, walks on and then comes back to smell it. As if she forgot the first time.

Lavender and coastal rosemary are planted along some paths, each with lovely purple flowers, and the woman occasionally rubs her fingers gently along a stem and smells them. She broke off a piece of rosemary once and took it home to use in cooking, but soon discovered it was not that kind of rosemary even though it smelt the same.

Certain flowers and trees seem to be favourites because she always stops, looks longer and takes more photos. Daises in all colours are everywhere and she looks closely at their different coloured centres, intricate shapes, stripes in some petals and any visiting bee. She thinks they are such happy plants. Flowering gum trees with their extraordinary gum blossoms seem to be a particular fascination. The multiple fluffy strands flow out from the gumnut after its lid falls off and the colours are glorious.

The woman stops for some dogs, talks to the owner and might take a photo of one. She nods her head at other people as they pass and occasionally makes a brief comment. Her walking is faster in the beginning and slower towards the end when she makes a scraping noise with one of her feet.

There are other times when the woman walks with the walker, pushing it forward as if it's a trolley loaded with goods doing a delivery. She could look like she was working. It could be a job sometimes to move against the wind tunnels on the streets running up from the water.

She has worn the same glasses for the last few years. They look like they have transition lenses. They're the expensive ones, aren't they? The man in the advertisement said to his mother wearing them, worried she was spending his inheritance. They are bright too, with orange sides and purple fronts with a slight orange tinge across the top of the frame.

The woman is never out when it rains or when the weather is bad. Although one very cold windy day she was, wearing a pale blue Hurtigruten wind jacket with the words *Greenland, Antarctica, Spitsbergen, Norway* in black letters written on the back. On rainy days she has been seen walking around large undercover carparks.

When the woman is out walking, she sometimes looks like she is really concentrating and her mouth changes shape. It could be a pout or just the lower lip coming up to cover the upper lip and being squeezed together. She does that, going uphill and also crossing the busy divided road with the palm lined strip in the middle. She has to judge the flow of traffic—the number of cars, how far away and how fast they were moving. There is a forty-kilometre speed limit in the residential area, but some vehicles don't seem to realise. Her mouth was covered with a mask later in the pandemic and the traffic was much less.

However, most times the woman looks curiously happy and content as she walks along looking around everywhere.

She is not overweight and could look fit and agile, if you saw her sitting. With her hat off, you can see her once dark brown hair has silver grey strands running through the new longer cropped hairdo.

On some paths you can hear her walker coming, especially if she is on the footpaths close to the water, where the tall apartment blocks are. Clop, clop—the walker's wheels make noises as they go over indentations running across at regular intervals. That sound annoys her a little.

Nevertheless, the woman who goes out walking loves the new footpaths. They are level, have ramps up and down from the road and flow easily through and around parks. The local council keeps them in good order and if any repairs are needed, the woman might report a hazard on the Snap Send Solve app on her phone.

The area that was once factories, warehouses and railway yards has been transformed over the last thirty years. The Beacon Cove development was finished before the old pier had its latest renovation. At one stage people were considering building apartments on the pier. The woman and other locals were thrilled when that didn't happen.

In the years before 2020, the woman was not seen out walking for a month or so, several times a year. But come 2020 with the pandemic, she was out more often. People were courteous and gave the woman plenty of space on the footpaths as they walked past. Council signs were up in several locations, reminding people to keep at least 1.5 metres apart.

By May 2020 she was on the other side of the big park where she hadn't been before, much further away than usual. The big park, Garden City Reserve, is part of an earlier community housing development in the 1920s. Later, during magpie swooping season in the park, she watched a bus going past again and noted the number, the entry door for accessibility, and thought she really must catch it one day and discover where it goes.

The council COVID cleaners were in the big park too during the pandemic, spraying and wiping posts and seats or picking up rubbish. It was the usual team of five or six, with the orange fluoro jackets moving inland after the sweep along the beachfront and pier. The woman often thanks them for cleaning as they move past.

The woman was also looking up more, listening to birds' calls and songs. She read bird sightings had increased and wondered about assisting conservation efforts by recording bird data. The Frog ID and My Pest Guide Reporter apps were already on her phone.

She also noticed police helicopters flying in the sky regularly during the pandemic while jets flew less and less. From the big park she could see the new Melbourne 108 building growing higher than the Eureka tower beside it, becoming the new tallest building in the city.

The woman heard more building noises as she walked, pylons being driven down in the new suburb next door. And within the less-new housing estate she could hear renovating sounds coming from inside— hammering, drilling and sanding.

Sometimes she walks back on the same path in the opposite direction and realises she sees things differently, the light falling at another angle, some flowers and different scenes stand out or looked better.

Occasionally, along the way, the woman sits and rests at the start of Monterey Walk, where she can see the path going to the small park of Beacon Square. The trees arch over the path and leaves transform over four seasons. During the pandemic she has seen the arrival of yellow, red and orange leaves in autumn, the bare trees in winter and hopes the flush of green in spring will come with improved COVID-19 numbers and the fully green leaves in summer might bring a new vaccine.

The nearby banksia tree is where twittering rainbow lorikeets peck into bits of the cones and she marvels at their bright red, yellow and green colours. The woman notes that they often fly down the nature corridor formed by the street to the beachfront where they have nests high in the palm trees.

Her thoughts follow the lorikeets down to Port Philip Bay and the two piers—places of new beginnings and travels past and planned.

With thoughts returned, the woman who goes out walking walks on, engrossed in nature close to home and enjoying extra time during COVID rules, doing more neighbourhood travel.

1. OFF TO TASMANIA (1973)

Two wharfies at Melbourne's Station Pier made a memorable start to our 1973 Tasmanian holiday. After arriving at the entry gate, the first wharfie frowned and shook his head, asking, 'Where are you nice girls going and why?'

'Tasmania. We're going to drive around for four weeks on holiday,' I answered happily and proudly. I didn't understand why he'd asked. After all, we were queued to drive onto the Princess of Tasmania, a ferry that only went to Tasmania. Where else would we be going?

Rosemary, Margaret, and I drove from Sydney in my pale blue VW beetle—with an old canvas tent—and planned to camp and travel around Tasmania. It was our summer holidays from university and my two friends, and I were looking forward to the trip. We thought Tasmania would be a fantastic place to visit.

He tried to change our minds.

'There's nothing there. You'd be better off staying here in Melbourne where there are bars and more things to do. It's dead down there at night.'

'No, we'll be fine. We need to get outdoors,' I told him.

Still shaking his head, he directed us ahead and told me to turn around, reverse the car down the ramp, and follow the next wharfie's instructions.

The second wharfie waved us on and directed me to a place in the ferry's hold so I could park alongside other cars. As we gathered our things, a loud bang sounded from the front of our car. Another car had reversed straight into us.

'What are you doing?' I asked the driver after I'd jumped out to look at the dent in the bonnet. I loved my first car, so I wasn't happy.

'Reversing, following the directions. He didn't say stop!' the man tried to explain.

I shook my head. How could it be the wharfie's fault?

My car was old, I had bought it second-hand, but it was still in good nick. The body had no dings (until then). The inside lining had disintegrated, but I'd patched that with adhesive contact vinyl sheets (black and white swirls, the latest rage). The little basic manual car did not have extra features, such as heating or cooling, but I loved it.

The VW's motor was in the rear, so I thought it shouldn't be damaged. The car would still drive okay. The driver said he didn't want to make a claim because it would affect his insurance and instead gave me some cash and told me it wouldn't cost much to fix the ding. I left it at that. We were on holiday.

That night, we tried to sleep in our seats on the Princess of Tasmania as she sailed over the rough Bass Strait. It wasn't very comfortable, but that didn't matter much to us. We were twenty and adventurous. We'd been on many camping trips and 'roughed it' on drives to Queensland and other places in coastal and outback New South Wales.

Rosemary and I went to the same high school for the first four years, and Margaret and I were boarders at another high school for the last two years. We had long, dark hair and looked like typical Australian university students in the 1970s: flared blue jeans (the latest craze to arrive from the USA), baggy tops (some of Indian design), sandals, patterned headscarves to hold our hair back and a few young freckles showing on our make-up free faces. We were happy to be away from study and casual employment.

The three of us were off to a new place, one we'd heard many wonderful things about—the wilderness, the unspoiled natural environment, an entire island to travel around and discover.

The next morning, we sailed into the Mersey River to dock at Devonport. It is the main port in the middle of the north coast of Tasmania. We grabbed a few tourist brochures from the ferry before driving off to explore. The car was going well and didn't experience another mishap in the hold.

The plan was to explore the north of Tasmania—around Devonport—before heading east in a clockwise direction. I wanted to drive to Southport before heading over to the remote and largely unexplored west coast before finding our way north again. We booked nothing in advance and the plan was not concrete.

Tasmania is a rough apple shape; 250 km across the middle and 300 km from north to south. That doesn't seem a large place to travel around, but Australia's smallest state is home to many hills, mountains, a lack of overtaking lanes, logging trucks, stunning scenery, and great national parks that make the drive slower.

About halfway down the east coast of Tasmania is Coles Bay. After driving over the corrugated dirt road—a by-road off the highway—that seemed like it went on forever, we set up our tent on the sandy shores of the bay. We saw no one else on the dirt road and there was no-no one else staying in the area we chose. We had the beach and the views of the pink granite peaks of the Hazards mountain range to ourselves. Coles Bay and the Freycinet Peninsula were true natural beauties. Sitting around the fire cooking our evening meal felt magical, only the stars in the sky and the Milky Way.

We'd heard about the spectacular Wineglass Bay on the ocean side of the Freycinet peninsula over the Hazards mountains. We also knew of a walk going straight up and down the mountain onto the beach and returning around the base.

One day, we began our trek with a haversack. I made sure we packed the haversack with items we could use in an emergency—an axe, rope, matches, newspaper, water, and similar bits and pieces.

The rocky granite route led to a lookout at the top of the mountain. The pack was heavy and getting to the mountain's peak was a steep climb.

I can recall the walk up very well. It was Rosemary and Margaret's birthday—they shared the same date in February. After carrying the pack for a while, Rosemary asked me, 'What on Earth have you got in this pack? It's so heavy.'

'Just a few things. In case we need them.'

'But the walk only takes a few hours, doesn't it?' Margaret joined in. 'We won't be out for long. It's not as if we're staying overnight.'

'You never know what might happen. It's best to be prepared,' I sheepishly answered. Perhaps I had packed too much. 'It must be my turn to carry it?'

The load was soon forgotten as we reached the top and saw the view. The beautiful Wineglass Bay lay in a crescent of white sand made of fine quartz, the bluest water forming a dramatic edge with its waves. The sun shone and the peninsula of sand, trees, and low bush and grasses extended further south to Mt Freycinet and Schouten Island. There were no people, and no noise, just glorious natural nature.

Freycinet National Park became the first national park established in Tasmania in 1916. Interestingly, the Peninsula and National Park are named after Louis de Freycinet, a French navigator who circumnavigated the earth and published the first map to show the full outline of Australia's coastline in 1811. Many French people visited Tasmania early in our colonial history, so quite a few places are named with French words.

We scrambled down the other side of the mountain to the sand on the beach. It was pristine, without a single footprint.

Before leaving the beach to take the level track back, we turned for one last look at the ocean. We couldn't believe our eyes when we saw a small penguin walking along the shoreline. It was an unbelievable sight. We didn't think anyone would believe us, but we saw the penguin.

I was worried the penguin was lost because it was alone. I naively thought it must've swum from Antarctica and be exhausted. I tried to think of something I could do to help and was about to go back, but it had disappeared. I don't know what I thought I'd be able to do. I later learnt there is a little penguin colony at Bicheno, just north of Wineglass Bay, and many penguin colonies exist along the Australian coastline. They don't all swim from Antarctica!

The walk through the bush to the waters of Coles Bay on the other side of the peninsula was hot work so, on the walk back, we stopped at one of the small, secluded bays we passed and jumped in for a swim.

Heavens knows what we wore, if anything. Maybe I'd packed our cozzies and towels in the haversack as well.

Being in crystal clear water was wonderful, cooling, and refreshing, and just what we needed. We also hadn't seen another person.

The walk was only meant to take a few hours. The map became unclear after we left the bay and headed inland. We couldn't see either the bay or the ocean in that thick, bushy area, and we passed only the occasional sign.

After an hour, we were still no closer to camp, and it was getting dark. I hoped I hadn't jinxed us with all the 'emergency gear' I'd packed.

When we saw the same sign more than once, we knew something wasn't right. At a fork in the track, we went in the opposite direction and finally saw lights. After much discussion about what had happened, we reached the old fisherman's pub on the bay—we'd noticed it in the distance before we went up the mountain earlier in the day. The shack of a hotel sat at the end of a dirt road with a small wharf onto Coles Bay. We were delighted to be at the pub. We told our story and had a beer.

We decided someone or something had turned the sign around along the last part of our walk.

Margaret taught us how to drink beer at pubs on the drive down from Sydney. Her parents ran hotels, and she introduced us to cheap pub meals and the occasional stop for a refreshing beer. She informed us of women's lounges, schooners, pints, and the like. I learned hotels, especially country pubs, were safe, friendly places and the Coles Bay pub was one of those.

At the bar, we decided it was too late to leave and cook our own dinner back at the tent and, starving, ate whatever was around. Foolishly, I hadn't packed food in the haversack.

That was a walk we'd never forget. Although it was supposed to take just a couple of hours, it took us all day. Deep down, I think we enjoyed most of it.

Several days later, we went on another walk, but we didn't love that one. The walk went beside Lake St Clair in another national park. That park was directly west from Coles Bay, in the middle of Tasmania.

To get there, we'd spent almost a week driving down via Hobart and Southport and up to the middle of the island.

The full Cradle Mountain walk was a six-day trek from one end to the other. We began our walk at the campgrounds of Lake St Clair and headed towards Cradle Mountain. The plan was to walk to the lakeside hut in one day, sleep the night, and then walk back on the same route the next day. I'm not sure why we started at the Lake St Clair end rather than the Cradle Mountain end. Maybe because Lake St Clair was the more level end, and no mountain climbing was necessary. But we didn't know about the mud.

Rosemary and I were girl guides and more than used to hiking and walking long distances, but Margaret wasn't into sports or exercise. She enjoyed reading more. I had no idea the eight-hour walking track trailed through ankle-deep mud along the lakeshore. We had to step up and over tangled tree roots. I thought at least we had no chance of getting lost as we trekked alongside the lake. The hard part was getting to and finding the hut before night fell.

'How much further? This is terrible,' Margaret called out as she drifted further and further behind us. 'Are you sure where we're going?'

No, I wasn't sure, but there was a dot on the map of the Cradle Mountain Lake St Clair National Park walking track.

Margaret slowly became a dot behind us, but we didn't lose sight of her as she stepped over the roots. She wasn't moving quickly, but it was enough to move her forward.

'I don't know exactly where we are, but there's a mark for the hut on the map's track just in from the lake's edge. It can't be much further.' I just wanted to reassure them because we couldn't see the track for all the mud. We also couldn't see any signs.

The trees and bush to our right were so thick at times we couldn't see the lake. The canopy was low too, and the ground was in darkness, void of sunlight.

But we made it to the hut before nightfall. It was rustic, and that's putting it kindly. It was a small log cabin with a tin roof and three sets of roughly hewn double bunks inside and not much else.

That night as we lay in bed, we heard all sorts of creepy-crawly sounds. We imagined enormous heavy spiders intermittently rushing or walking. We teased each other by making similar noises on the wooden walls on one side of our beds with our fingers. That lead to shrieks and cries of fright and alarm and made us laugh so much we could hardly get off to sleep. Then the Tasmanian devils started fighting. It sounded like multiple murders taking place at the same time, right outside the cabin's front door.

It was so dark. We had no electricity and limited amenities, like the one cold-water tap outside. We didn't even have a toilet, but we must have gone somewhere. That night we all went into a wonderful exhausted deep sleep.

The next day, we spotted a fishing boat on the lake. It travelled in the direction of the camping grounds.

'Let's wave it down and get a lift back,' someone said. 'It'll save us having to walk that track again.'

I ran out to the edge of the lake and waved vigorously. Two people in the boat waved back, then continued, waving. We waited a little while, but they didn't come over. They were just waving hello back to us. We didn't see another boat after that.

'Looks like we have to walk back,' someone said with disappointment.

The lake was beautiful, and the forest and bush were very natural, but the mud we walked in for kilometres wasn't enjoyable. The walk back seemed shorter and less of a hassle because we knew what it would be like. We were alone on the walk again, so we laughed and talked our way back to camp, ready to move on.

We made good time and left the campsite in the middle of the day, pleased to be back on the road again and heading west.

My old VW beetle had NSW number plates. Whenever another car passed us on the road, people waved, and we waved back. We were visitors and, thus, novelties. The greetings we received made us feel welcome, safe, and happy.

We may have been a novelty, but my aunt was even more so. She cycled her way around Tasmania on her own in the late 1940s. She'd knocked on farmhouse doors and featured in the local newspapers. What an amazing thing to do at the time.

Aunty Clare had spoken about the welcoming people of Tasmania and all the fruit growing alongside the road free for picking. The friendly attitude and the fruit were still there. We picked fresh blackberries, mulberries, raspberries, and, of course, the occasional apple.

Tasmania was famous for apple growing and we saw orchards everywhere. The odd tree grew outside the fence line on the side of the road and pulling over without traffic to eat delicious fruit was so easy. And free.

The other discoveries we found were Devonshire tea and the CWA (Country Women's Association) tearooms. Along the roads, we often saw signs advertising Devonshire Tea. We stopped so many times (too many) for scones with jam, cream and a cup of tea. If we didn't see a Devonshire tea sign, we'd look for a CWA building to get a free cup of tea with a biscuit.

Tasmania was (and still is) an amazing place. Everyone was sociable and generous. It wasn't only the locals but also other visitors.

A fellow on a motorbike overtook us driving up the remote west coast and waved us down. He presented us with one of the lobsters he'd caught that morning following his night on a fishing trawler. He was travelling and working his way around Australia, noticed us at a campsite and thought we might like one. Sadly, these days one is warier when getting waved down.

After many thanks, we never saw him again. We thought lobster was such a special item of food, that we rented an on-site caravan for the night with a kitchen and a dining table.

We were young, free, and independent. We could go to any place we wanted whenever we chose. We were responsible for only ourselves. Living, laughing, experiencing, learning, appreciating, and in charge of our own lives.

Only recently, it struck me how lucky we were and still are in Australia.

I once listened to an academic speak about her research on child marriages and how it affects women. I knew child marriages happened, but I didn't know the statistics and the countries that were involved. Hearing how often it happened frightened me and I can't imagine what it must be like for someone else to decide for a young girl, a woman, or anyone for that matter, based on culture, monetary reward, religion, or family expectations. When it is because they're female, the inequality of it all is astounding. We were so lucky to be born in Australia to parents who placed no such expectations or rigid rules for our future.

I've been back to Tasmania many times and I still love the place, but there have been changes.

Once, when I was in Hobart for work in 2003, I visited an area of land that was set aside for re-development in the inner-city suburb of Sandy Bay. The site was on the upper side of a hill that looked down onto the Derwent River and Wrest Point Casino on the shoreline. Wrest Point Casino was Australia's first legal casino and, at seventeen stories high, it really stood out. The casino opened in February 1973 and had just been built when I first visited.

To my surprise, the re-development site was once the local council's public camping ground, Peel St Caravan Park. That was where I'd camped when I first visited Hobart thirty years earlier.

Being in that location again and to see the campsite was long gone was strange.

Times had changed. The suburb had grown; it had become very fashionable and had some of the most expensive real estate in Hobart. It thrilled me to know that a complex of aged care facilities would be built on the side of that hill. The people living there would have the best views. It seems they often leave views out of aged care facilities, but it's important. I'd want a view.

Coles Bay has changed too. Million-dollar resorts are built not far from our old campsite, and they charge about $1,000 a night. The old dirt road in from the highway is paved and buses regularly take tourists along it. Houses have popped up in the area along with resorts and hotels. The Freycinet National Park is still there, but the walk up the hill has been upgraded. It is now marked with rocks and steps, neatly arranged, to save the scrambling.

Wineglass Bay has been voted one of the world's top ten beaches. They have added permanent signs explaining the natural environment and history of the area. Directional signs are planted solidly in the ground and can't be turned in the opposite direction.

On the other hand, Lake St Clair has changed very little. A national park visitor's centre is now situated near where we camped.

Years ago, we camped on the lake's edge, but camping is now prohibited that close to the lake. The campground is back where the road leaves the highway.

I've only recently learned Lake St Clair is the deepest lake in Australia and forms the headwaters for the Derwent River flowing down through Hobart into the Tasman Sea. The lake is still pristine.

The surrounding area of Cradle Mountain Lake St Clair National Park has become a popular tourist destination. More sophisticated huts have been built along the six-day walking trail. The walk, now known as the Overland Track, is world famous. The track passes through some of the finest mountain terrains and includes ancient forests and glacial lakes. They have built boardwalks to protect mosses, ferns, and other delicate plants. The days of deep mud treading and harming the environment have gone.

The national park is within the Tasmanian wilderness World Heritage Area (WHA) making up about twenty percent of Tasmania. The Tasmanian devil features in posters at Lake St Clair, while at the Cradle Mountain end there is a Tasmanian devil wildlife sanctuary. I can still hear the screams!

Much of the southwest of Tasmania has not been explored, while other areas are only open to limited foot traffic. Some parts are tough to get to. These days helicopter flights or boat trips to isolated bays along the coast are the only way to access them.

My appreciation of Tasmania continues to grow, especially now that new species of plants are still being discovered.

In 1973, at the end of our time on the 'Apple Isle', we caught the ferry back from Devonport to Melbourne. I didn't see the two wharfies at Station Pier to tell them what a fantastic trip we'd had.

We'd spent our money until we were left with only five cents between us as we drove back into Sydney.

I still have my photographic slides. However, they don't show the times I remember most. I must have been enjoying myself so much that I forgot to take photos. I have never forgotten Tasmania and can't wait to go back there again.

Postscript

I took my car to a garage upon returning home. When I showed the ding to the panel beater, he lifted the bonnet and, with one kick, he popped the dent out, leaving no sign of damage.

'You can pocket that cash the fellow gave you. No more work needed.'

2. THE TONGARIRO ALPINE CROSSING (2000)

We went to New Zealand with no intention of doing that trek. But we went to walk and walk we did. In two weeks, we covered more than 70 kilometres on both the north and south islands. But the Tongariro Crossing wasn't on our list.

It all started in a map shop. We had some maps for walks we'd planned but were missing others. Somewhere, driving south on the North Island towards Lake Taupo, I spotted a good-looking map shop in a small town. It stood out because there weren't many other shops nearby and you don't often come across map shops.

'Quick, Sue, look over there. Let's stop and check it out.'

We were surprised to find that the shop had so many different kinds of maps, including 3D. We told the shopkeeper we were looking for a walking map of the Abel Tasman Walk, on the tip of the South Island.

We were planning to go there after the Queen Charlotte walk nearby. A great conversation followed. He was passionate about walking, as we were, and we chatted happily with him.

He asked us, sounding confused, 'But why would you want a map of the Abel Tasman when the greatest one-day walk in the world is only a few kilometres from here?'

'What walk is that?'

'Tongariro Crossing. It's spectacular.'

'I've never heard of that.'

'Really? It's famous. People come from all over the world to do the walk. It's past volcanoes, over moonscape, and has a stunning view from the top. Definitely the best one-day walk in New Zealand.'

He had our full attention.

'Here's a map. Most people do the walk one way. A bus drops you off at the beginning and another one picks you up at the end. But you have to be outside the information centre at Whakapapa early in the morning for the pickup. Here's the information.'

The more the man told us about the walk, the more we both thought we just had to do it. We hadn't booked anywhere to stay for the next few days, so we bought the walking maps and headed for Mt Ruapehu and Whakapapa. I love the name of some of those New Zealand towns. Oh, and it was 'tramping' that we were doing, not walking, in New Zealand speak.

As we drove there, I told Sue about the amazing place I'd visited with my family on our New Zealand trip when I was fifteen. On our bus tour we had a day at leisure, somewhere near or at Lake Taupo. Mum had read about Mt Ruapehu and seen photos of people swimming in the warm lake at the top of the volcano. They were surrounded by snow, and she wanted to see it. My adventurous mother organised a taxi to take us all to Mt Ruapehu for a few hours' drive. It was an amazing side trip. As well as the volcano, we stopped to look at a gorgeous grand old hotel called Chateau Tongariro. It had a small golf course in front and mountains behind. I never forgot the sight of it.

One of my travel fantasies was to go back one day and stay there. So that was exactly where we went first to find accommodation for a few nights. The hotel was booked out for the first night but available for two nights after that. We booked for then.

For the first night, we found a vacancy at a ski lodge hotel higher up the mountain which operated all year round. Staying there felt like old times from my days of skiing on some weekends in Perisher Valley in New South Wales. I couldn't afford to stay in ski resorts but going inside one to order a drink and look around was another fantasy experience.

To do the Tongariro Crossing walk safely required a bit of planning, as it is weather dependent. It was important to pick a clear day with a calm blue sky. Although it was summer, the weather could turn and become dangerous, we were told. The weather prediction for the next day was not good, and we were advised to do a shorter walk closer to accommodation and wait until the following day to do the main crossing walk.

The next morning, we went to the information centre at Whakapapa for advice and more maps. The centre was near the Whakapapa Village, between the two volcanoes of Mt Ruapehu and Mt Ngauruhoe.

There were a number of walks in the area to choose from. We chose a four to six hour walk across alpine grasses and hills the next day. It wasn't the right day for walking higher in the mountains because it was misty at ground level and clouds filled the sky.

I remember finishing that shorter walk about 100 metres behind Sue. I used to wear the backpack walking because Sue had a bad knee and I thought it would help if I took the load. Coming up that last rise felt exhausting. In a video Sue took of me, my face looks tired. I thought at the time that it was the heavy backpack.

A few hours later we had recovered and by then we were staying at the chateau eating a nice dinner with wine to help. We went to bed early because the following day, if the weather was fine, we would need to start early to finish the Tongariro Crossing in daylight.

The next day was indeed fine. 'Look, I can see the top of Mt Ngauruhoe today. Quick Sue, look out the window,' I said. We dressed quickly, had breakfast and then walked up to the Whakapapa information centre to wait for the bus. Before too long there was quite a crowd waiting. Buses came and went, dropping people off, and the queue grew.

I learned later that buses operated back at Lake Taupo and other places, a long way away, to bring people in to do the walk. From listening to everyone chat, there seemed to be many nationalities going on this walk.

The bus went off the highway along a dirt road to the bottom of the Mangatepopo Valley. We were dropped off in a car park at the very end of the unsealed road. We had a valley and a mountainside to climb immediately ahead of us.

Our maps were not all that detailed, but there were enough people doing the walk around us, so it wasn't difficult to find our way.

Sue and I walked up the valley, following the trail near the Mangatepopo Stream. We walked along the edges of old lava flows to reach the first steep climb up the lowermost side of Mt Ngauruhoe (2291 metres at its highest point). It was up over rocks big and small and took quite some time. Gee, that was a steep climb for me. I was used to walking up and down hills, but not rock climbing up the side of steep mountains.

Near the top of the climb people were gathering together, looking concerned. They kept turning their heads skywards. Not towards the active volcanoes but into the blue sky. We kept moving up further and when we reached the top of the climb onto a flat plateau, we stopped to rest. I asked others resting nearby about the group of concerned-looking people. They told me a man had fallen and broken his arm and paramedics were coming to collect him by helicopter. A doctor and a nurse had already stopped to give assistance.

After a short rest, we strode across the flat plateau. About a kilometre in we could hear and see the helicopter flying away after collecting the man. As I looked back and up, I saw the steep upper side of Mt Ngauruhoe leading to the peak. A couple of people were climbing and sliding back down the gravelly surface. That was an optional side trip noted on the guide map. But it said allow an extra three hours to get up and back and be prepared for advancing three paces and coming back two. We didn't want to do that side trip.

The firm grey volcanic silt plateau was level, which made walking across to the next smaller climb feel like a walk in the park compared to our earlier climbs.

In 2000, I was at the height of enjoying long walks. I enjoyed all types of walking, checking out fresh places, looking at the bush or countryside and especially looking at wonderful views. Walking with Sue was especially joyful. We loved walking together. But she was always much faster. Everyone who walked with Sue commented on how much trouble they had keeping up. I only just managed.

After the next short climb, we headed towards a volcano.

The whole walk was fabulous, and it is hard to pick the best moments, but three aspects of the Tongariro Crossing walk stood out for me. The first, walking up to and along the edge of an active volcano and looking down inside it at the red-hot lava bubbling up and down was incredible. The sides of the Red Crater of Mt Tongariro from the top at 1886 metres were brown-red, cakey and sheer. As I stretched to peer over the edge, I remember thinking–there is no protective rail here, I could just fall in! Or the side could give way! I moved away before too long.

Then walking down, or rather sliding down, from the active volcano I saw the next remarkable scene. There were two or three pools of coloured water or small lakes at different levels. The colours of milky blues and greens standing out from the grey ash were otherworldly. Some were steaming with their chemical mix, whilst others of the Emerald Lakes were just sitting there in all their glorious, colourful display.

Sitting beside one of the small lakes, we stopped to have our lunch. Other walkers had also stopped for lunch or a break. I don't recall hearing any conversations or voices. There was a silence as if we were all in another world and just stunned. Time to just sit and wonder for a while with everyone lost in their own thoughts.

After finishing our rolls, we continued the walk. We went up a few more small hills, one that seemed to be like a sand hill. The material under my feet was very difficult to get a hold on to move upwards. But I made it and the walk soon went around another larger lake where the water looked a more normal blue colour. There was a sign saying it was safe to swim.

From there it was downhill all the way to the base. But it wasn't a quick descent. It took hours and hours to wind our way down along the path. The third amazing scene then appeared before our eyes. We saw it in the distance ahead of us for at least an hour before it went away. Then as we came around the mountain, it appeared again briefly before finally disappearing with our descent into tropical ferny groves and cool trickling streams.

It was a beautiful lake. If it was Lake Taupo, we must have been high up to look out and see the whole lake! That lake in the centre of the North Island of New Zealand extends over almost 50 kilometres. Could we have seen that? Perhaps it was the smaller lake, Lake Rotoaira, which was closer to us. I've looked at many maps and I still can't work out which one it was. Regardless, it was a fantastic view to accompany us on our descent. Going down was easier too.

About halfway down, we passed sacred Maori grounds. Hot steam rose out from vents in the earth along the hillsides, adding to the otherworldliness of it all.

The rich green landscape of most of the New Zealand we'd seen so far, only appeared at the end of the walk. It wasn't lush grass pastures but lush green tropical plants on the wetter, sunnier side of the mountain range. All the landscapes along the walk were different. Approaching the first climb it was an alpine terrain of tiny waterways, mosses and grasses with a small waterfall thrown in. The trail winding gradually upwards changed to large and small rocks piled almost vertically. The volcanoes with old volcanic ash and active lava were on the top with coloured chemical lakes. The descent was steep, but not as vertical as at the start, and had almost paddock-like hillsides, albeit with some steam vents and then the tropical forest at the base.

It took us about nine hours to get up across the range and down to the base on the other side where there were a few buses already waiting. We caught one back to Whakapapa to stay one more night at the Chateau Tongariro.

Wow, what a wonderful day. It was the best one-day walk I have ever done.

We left the North Island the next day, driving south to Wellington and then boarding a ferry to Picton in the north of the South Island.

There were two more walks in the South Island after that, and they were much longer. We walked a three-day section of the Queen Charlotte track that was magnificent and then another three-day component of the Abel Tasman walk.

All up we'd walked about 75 kilometres in two weeks in New Zealand. But I kept getting slower towards the end of each walking day, sometimes tripping over.

Over the next 12 months, my walking gradually became much more difficult. At the end of 2001, I saw a neurologist and had an MRI scan that showed I had a demyelinating disease that had probably been there for some time. My secondary progressive MS (multiple sclerosis) wasn't diagnosed until 2006.

Most aspects of my life changed after that. But my passion for travel has always continued. It became even more important to do as much as I could, as fast as I could, before things got even worse!

I travel a lot now with whatever gear I need to help me. The mobility aids have improved with time, and I try to keep up to date with what the latest is. I am also choosing more challenging trips to far and away places. I can leave the softer, easier travels until I'm less mobile.

But the Tongariro Crossing walk will always be in my mind and heart. I loved doing that walk. I did that walk with Sue when my legs were walking well. I still walk with Sue, but I've got it easier now and I'm faster on my Luggie mobility scooter! No problems keeping up.

3. JAPANESE TRAINS (2014)

The trouble started at the train station next to Kansai International Airport. It was 2014 and our first visit to Japan. When we landed in Osaka in the evening, we knew exactly where we had to go and how to get there. But that didn't make it as easy as we thought it would be.

We knew it was a short walk to the airport rail station. We also knew we needed to catch the Japan Rail (JR) train to our hotel, located in the building over Shin-Osaka rail station. Finding the first station wasn't hard. But upon entering it, the number of train routes and destinations displayed on numerous signs above the ticket machines dazzled me. And JR was only one of many different train operators.

People were rushing around and getting their tickets from a myriad of machines. Stunned, I just sat on my scooter, staring with my mouth open.

'Let's get a ticket', Sue said as she moved towards the vending machines. I wasn't sure we'd be able to get the correct one in time, and there weren't many trains going to Shin-Osaka at the late hour we arrived, so I convinced Sue to go to the ticket office instead. That was the first mistake we made with the Japanese trains.

We had about twenty minutes to buy the tickets and find the correct platform to catch the next train. Plenty of time, I thought. We didn't see any trains inside the station building, just turnstile entrances to platforms somewhere. We moved past the vending machines and into the adjacent ticket office. I went into one of the queues riding my small scooter. Sue followed, pulling our suitcase on wheels. Soon we were at the counter to buy our tickets. The trip was supposed to take fifty minutes, with just two stops on the fast train.

A simple request, I thought, with Japanese cash in hand. I added that I would take the scooter on the train with me.

The man behind the counter became quite confused. 'Ohh, ooh, I will find out', he said. He went to an office area behind him and after a few minutes came out with another man and woman. I explained we wanted to buy two tickets for the next train to Shin-Osaka and I would ride my scooter to the train carriage, then collapse it down and take it aboard with me. In response, there was much conversation and consternation in Japanese. Then one of them said, 'you cannot go on the JR train here. You will have to go to another station and get all stations train'.

'Why? What's the problem?' I asked. Sue had been patiently standing by and listening until she heard the next response.

'You cannot go on any JR train.'

'Where is the other station?' Sue asked.

'It is one to two hours away.'

'How do we get there?'

'There is a bus outside the airport.'

Then I chipped in, 'How long will the other train take to get to Shin-Osaka?'

'Two hours.'

I exploded, 'We want to take the direct train. And we have paid for JR passes. We are going to spend the next two weeks catching trains all over Japan.'

Then one of the attendants said, 'No, too big.'

I jumped off the scooter and stood holding on to its tiller. 'No,' I said, 'look, I can get off, and it collapses down'. Then folding down the back of the seat, I indicated that the seat goes right down too, 'see it all goes down' undoing and bringing the tiller down as well.

'Not enough room on the train.'

'Sue, let's collapse it all the way down.'

'It's only the same size as a suitcase. See how small it gets.'

'Mmm,' then followed with more Japanese sounding noises of perhaps some understanding. After further discussion amongst them, the two other people who came out returned to the back office and the man at the counter prepared the tickets.

I looked at the big clock on the wall, the time getting closer and closer to our train's departure. The number of people queuing to buy tickets had dwindled. It was getting late, and I was tired and anxious.

We left home at 3:15am to get to Melbourne Airport to catch a flight to Cairns, then another to Osaka. It was about 9pm when we arrived at Kansai.

After taking some time to organise our tickets, the attendant finally handed them over. As we turned around to leave, the people from the office came out again. 'Please, the tickets,' one man said with his hand outstretched. They took our tickets and disappeared back into the office for a long time. There was hardly anyone around outside with us.

'We'll miss our train,' I said to Sue.

She spoke firmly to the attendant, 'give us our tickets back please. We have to catch the train.'

The man from the office came out and crossed the tickets over his chest. 'No, no go. Not with that.'

'What is the problem?' I exclaimed.

Another traveller suddenly appeared and offered to help. He was a Japanese man in his thirties who spoke excellent English with a slight North American accent. He told us he grew up in Japan, but now worked in the US and was here visiting family. 'What's happening?' he asked. We explained, and he spoke to the train attendants to find out what the problem was.

'They don't want you to ride the scooter on the platforms or anywhere on the station for the JR trains. It is against regulations.'

'That's ridiculous,' I said. 'What are they worried about? What do people in wheelchairs do? Don't they let people in electric wheelchairs use the trains?'

There didn't seem to be a straightforward answer to my questions. The man helping us couldn't work it out either. Time was passing, and we missed our train. I noted there was one last train that evening in about fifty minutes. We had to catch that one.

'What is so special about the JR trains? Do they go so fast that there is a problem? Do the doors open and shut at such a speed that we'll be crushed?' Was this was going to be a problem for our holiday in Japan?

Once again Sue told them, 'We're here for three weeks, on holiday, and we'll be catching trains all over Japan.'

'Who did the booking? What agency are you organised with?'

'It's booked with Peregrine.' I told them and they all looked back at me blankly.

I started to demonstrate how the scooter collapsed again when Sue suggested I give up doing that. They'd already seen it, and it didn't help.

'Do you think they are worried I might run into people inside the station? Is it an occupational health and safety thing they have a problem with? Or maybe there are so many people moving that they think someone will run into me and be hurt?' Unable to work it out, we were going around in circles not getting anywhere. We'd been there for well over an hour.

Sick of all this kerfuffle, Sue said, 'We are going to catch the next JR train. Give us our tickets back.'

Suddenly, several rail attendants from outside arrived in the middle of all this confusion, one with a wheelchair. He pointed for me to get in and the man behind the counter gave Sue our tickets.

'I'm not letting these out of my hands,' Sue softly said to me.

The man with the wheelchair moved closer. 'I'm not getting in that wheelchair. I have my own. This is not an airport, is it? And what will happen to my scooter?'

It seemed Sue had to wheel the collapsed scooter and our one bag and walk with a man wheeling me in a wheelchair.

'No, we're not doing that. How can my friend wheel that and the bag at the same time? This is ridiculous, we're going.' We were intent on just getting out of there and onto that last train. I rode my scooter and Sue wheeled our suitcase. As we left the ticket area, the Japanese man from the US was waiting for us.

'I'll help you find the right platform,' he said. 'Follow me'.

'Do you understand what that was all about?' I asked him.

'They have these rules they have to follow. I don't know much about scooters or wheelchairs.'

I gathered the best way to get to the train now was to blend in and try not to look obvious. A bit of hiding was the way to go, I thought.

At the ticket turnstiles, I had to go through an area for people with walking aids. A station attendant was looking at everyone's tickets. Somehow, we made it through, and no one stopped us.

'Quick let's get to the train while the going is good,' I said, as I sped off.

I felt as I imagined a criminal might feel trying to escape. There weren't many people at the station at that time of night, and there wasn't a problem getting to the platform. There were lifts and signs in English and numbers as figures we understood everywhere.

We made it to the correct platform with five minutes to spare. A guard on the platform in a blue uniform and cap, wearing white gloves and holding a whistle in one hand and a flag in the other, approached us. 'Oh no' I thought. By then I was standing to stretch my legs. He walked past us without a word or look.

I had instructions from the hotel as to which train to catch and in what direction, and how to get to the hotel from where we were to get off. The indicator panel lit up, showing the next train was going to Shin-Osaka.

It was an ordinary train, not particularly fast at all. We rolled and lifted the collapsed scooter in, and I walked with my two walking sticks. The scooter fitted into an open luggage area and we easily found seats in the mostly empty train carriage.

It was a fifty-minute journey to Shin-Osaka. The movement of the train lulled me into a meditative world and time passed quickly. We got off the train at the second stop and rolled and lifted the scooter and luggage out onto the platform. We weren't there long before two train guards approached. I was surprised when they said, 'We are here to help you. Where are you going? They rang and told us you were on the train.'

'Thank you. The Remm Shin-Osaka Hotel, please.'

'We will take you there.' I couldn't believe the service and attention we were receiving. There was no objection to me riding the scooter through the station.

They put the luggage on a trolley and walked with us, showing us the way, taking many turns left and right. Everywhere looked clean, bright and full of life, even though it was 11pm. We went past a big sign for the Shinkansen (bullet train) line and soon saw the hotel entrance with 'Remm' in bright lights.

Train stations in Australia were nothing like this. This was a huge, undercover conglomeration of multiple shopping centres, arcades, shops, restaurants, passageways and takeaway food outlets on many levels.

When we got to the hotel entrance, we thanked the train guards. They bowed and smiled and went back to the station.

We caught the elevator to reception on Level 12. Our room was on the 16th floor of 17 and was ultra-modern. Large windows gave an open view of the city and the bathroom had glass walls with blinds. It was on the small side, but excellent.

We made it. Thank goodness. What a story.

'I'll ask the Japanese guide when we meet up with her tomorrow, see if she knows what the problem could have been at the beginning.'

'I have no idea what they were on about. I'm bushed. Let's go to sleep,' Sue said.

When I asked our guide the next morning, she didn't understand either. She had tickets and seats, and we caught trains in the usual way over the next few days.

Then things changed.

We were first stopped at the gate of a station going through the disabled access. 'Do you have a booking?' We looked at our guide. She said no, and a long conversation in Japanese followed. 'Stop, wait here,' was our final instruction.

'What's happening?' I asked our guide.

'I didn't make any disabled bookings. I wasn't sure what your scooter looked like.'

'But I sent photos of the scooter when I was doing the booking.'

'They didn't send them to me. I thought I'd wait and see what you and it looked like.'

'Okay. And why are we waiting here? I thought you said the train was leaving at a certain time and we only had a few minutes to spare.'

'They are going to get a wheelchair.'

'But I don't need a wheelchair. I just want to ride my scooter to the train. What will happen to my scooter?'

'They will send a trolley for it. You better collapse it down.'

'I will have to stand and wait then. I can't see a seat anywhere. There's steps over there, I can sit on one.' I was getting cranky again at not being allowed to use my scooter. I didn't understand. We collapsed the scooter down and I sulked over to the steps and sat down.

We waited more than a few minutes. Then four men arrived in train guard uniform, all with white gloves. One had a wheelchair, one had a big wooden trolley on wheels, one had a walkie-talkie and one just seemed to observe. I got in the wheelchair; the scooter went on to the trolley and then we all went off, led by the man observing. His first job I realised was to find the elevator and push the button.

Only the man who pressed the button, the man pushing me, and the wheelchair could fit in the elevator. The man with the trolley with my scooter on it had to wait till the lift returned. Sue, the bag and our guide found their way to the platform led by the man with the walkie-talkie.

When we arrived on the platform yet another man in uniform arrived to help. His job was to use his key to open a small metal door where a ramp was stored inside. He took the ramp out. A sixth man in an even fancier uniform also joined us. I was sitting in a wheelchair waiting for a train with six train attendants to help me. I had to laugh.

Our ticket stated the numbers for our service, carriage and seat. The numbers of the carriage with the associated line to stand behind were all signposted, and the path was marked clearly. Time was counting down, and the train was coming soon, but the man with the trolley with my scooter on had not arrived yet. The man with the walkie-talkie was talking.

'Where's my scooter?' I asked, feeling helpless. All I could do was sit there and let it happen. Whatever happened, I supposed there would be another train and it wouldn't really be the end of the world. And we had a Japanese-speaking guide to help, too.

Announcements and musical noises were playing out of speakers. The train was coming. Look out! As the train approached the man with the trolley appeared panting and out of breath. I was still surrounded by five guards with my scooter now not far behind me. All I could do was smile.

Me smiling at Japanese trains

We waited our turn to enter the carriage. The man with the ramp laid it carefully from the platform onto the train, level with no gradient over a minimal gap. I walked over it with my two walking sticks. The scooter, bags, Sue and our guide followed, all assisted by the guards.

There was a disabled seat with a tiny space beside it where the scooter didn't fit. I learned they made the space for a small manual foldup wheelchair. We rolled the scooter onto the floor under our feet and put our feet on top. We were all inside the high-speed train, ready for take-off with more than a few minutes to spare. The train left on time.

What an incredible experience. I couldn't believe so many people had to be involved. All those people employed.

I felt a range of conflicting emotions–grateful for the help but annoyed I wasn't allowed to be independent; impressed by the number of people helping but struck by the inefficiency and waste of manpower. I was confused and didn't understand.

We chatted with our guide about people with disabilities in Japan and people in wheelchairs.

'They don't go out. They stay inside,' she told us. I hadn't noticed anyone moving about independently in a wheelchair or on a scooter during our travels in Japan.

'Why? What is the problem?'

'People with disabilities, or who are old and frail with mobility problems, live with their families. People with problems don't want to worry other people to take them out. That's the way they're brought up. That's what they've been taught.'

'Oh dear, that doesn't sound right.'

'The other thing about Japanese people is their culture, where they believe it is more important to help people than watch or let them help themselves. They must help.'

'But independence is an important thing. I want to be independent. I want to take myself.'

'Yes, well that's a big difference, and it is only in recent times, with younger Japanese people with disabilities speaking out, that some things in Japan are changing.'

It was interesting chatting, but there were views out the train window and I wanted to see the Japanese countryside. More about this helping business later.

I was surprised by the number of small rice fields beside houses or in the middle of a group of houses. Sure, the cities were packed full of high-rise buildings, but out of the cities people were living simpler lives. They were planting and picking their own rice, growing and sharing their own vegetables. It was different to what I expected.

We had a kaiseki dinner that night and the freshness, flavour and intricate arrangement was unique. Japanese food is incredibly good and healthy to boot.

Over dinner, (in between instructions of what to have what with) we returned to discussing how people with mobility problems in Japan manage the trains. Our guide told us about her friend Miwa. Miwa is 62 years old and had used a wheelchair for the last 30 years. She contracted polio when she was a child. Miwa belonged to a group of wheelchair users who were advocates for making improvements for people with disabilities.

Apparently in 1987, Miwa learned about a plan to build a new railway station in Fukuoka, Japan. At the time people in wheelchairs 'had to beg for help to be carried up and down stairs' as railway stations didn't have elevators. Whenever it was suggested elevators be installed, some argued they weren't needed. Railway staff were there to help people using wheelchairs by carrying them on stairs or to the toilet. When the station at Fukuoka was being rebuilt Miwa and her friends got together.

The group of campaigners organised large numbers of people in wheelchairs to go to railway stations on specific days at the same time across Japan. Railway staff tried to move people up and down stairs, quickly, and were overwhelmed by the large numbers. They called the campaign, 'We Go By Trains' and it became a nationwide movement. It showed that people with a disability want to live independently. Because of this work, many railway stations in Japan now have elevators and accessible toilets.

Miwa's passion for equal accessibility on public transport was really a fight for a human right from which many will benefit. But there was still a problem. Sure, there were now lifts at train stations, but I wasn't allowed to use them independently. The train station attendants still wanted to help!

'It's our culture,' our guide reminded me again. It's more important for Japanese people to help others than let them help themselves. She then said Miwa's next campaign was to point out the importance of independence and ask authorities, 'Why do you think we need or want help?'

Another aspect of Japan that struck me was how isolated from the outside world it could be. Closed in many ways. For a country I thought would be at the forefront of innovation and technology, an idea of mine based on all its electrical devices in the past, I was surprised when I went to visit the Museum of Emerging Science and Innovation (Miraikan) in Tokyo.

I went in on my scooter and up to where the robots were about to come out for a show. A museum attendant stopped me. 'No, you cannot be here on that. You have to get off.'

'I can't.' I got the attention of our guide and asked her to help.

'What's wrong?'

'He says I can't use my scooter in here.' Our guide talked with the attendant.

'He thinks it's a child's toy and you can't use it here.'

'Tell him it's my wheelchair. I can't get around without it. I'm not using it for fun.'

'I know, I'll explain to him you have a disability, and this is your electric wheelchair.' As our guide was telling the attendant this, and it took some time to explain to him, his expression changed completely.

His mouth fell open in shock and he shook his head. He said he had seen nothing like it before. And there I was with robots about to come out behind me and creatures that moved when spoken to, and my scooter seemed beyond understanding.

Of all the countries I'd been to, no one had ever been shocked like he was. No wonder the train staff had problems when I first arrived. They didn't have a clue what I was talking about. All of us were surprised.

Japan is wonderful to visit but difficult to get your head around on a first trip. At the end of our travels, I was still trying to work out how the Japanese train system worked for people with disabilities. I suppose I'll just have to return to keep figuring it out.

4. A BIKE SHOP IN COPENHAGEN (2015)

I thought I'd experienced everything that could go wrong travelling with my mobility scooter. But the events in Copenhagen in mid-2015 topped them all.

We booked a trip leaving Copenhagen to join an expedition cruise aboard the MS Fram. This time, the Hurtigruten ship would sail down the west of Greenland, visiting many of the spectacular sights and small towns on the coast. We arrived in Copenhagen a week early to catch up with our good friend Robin, who flew from London to meet us.

It was my first time in Copenhagen. We stayed in an apartment hotel near the cruise ship terminal on the northern side of the city. It wasn't far from the famous Little Mermaid statue on the harbour and was close to the Østerport train station.

Our city map had several walking trails marked with red footsteps. After a few days of taking a different route each time, we made it to the square beside the town hall. We had been walking for about four hours in the heat and it was time to change my scooter battery and take advantage of the public toilets in the shade.

When I rode out of the disabled toilet, I suggested to Sue we change the battery there, where it was cool. At that point, the scooter stopped anyway; the battery was flat.

'This battery seems stuck,' said Sue, sounding perplexed. 'Did you see how Wendy got it out when you had the new part fitted?'

'No. Wendy didn't explain anything about the new part. You picked it up for me on the way home from golf. I thought she would have shown you how it worked.'

The new part was a new base with a different method to hold and connect the battery. The old damaged base used Velcro straps. The new base had a small spring-loaded piece that came out.

'Wendy said to put the battery in first, then push it down until you hear a click.'

'But what about taking it out?'

'I thought you just pulled it up,' said Sue, doing exactly that. We both heard the snapping sound as the piece broke off, leaving nothing to hold the battery in place. There was a small piece of rigid plastic lying on the floor.

I put the second battery in, but there was no connection. Sue thought she'd see if the little piece on the floor fitted in the battery rather than the scooter. She tried to fit it and it disappeared inside a hole, never to come out again. It just made a rattling sound when we shook the battery.

We pushed the scooter out and I waited while Sue and Robin went to the tourist information office for help.

I was waiting more than an hour and wondered what had happened to them. It was getting hotter, and I pushed the scooter closer to the town hall or Rådhus for shade. I read my tourist guide and saw I was in a large central square called Rådhuspladsen, a landmark in the heart of Copenhagen.

A popular pedestrian shopping street, Strøget, and a historic fun park, Tivoli Gardens, were adjacent. I wondered if my two friends had opted for either the 'pleasure garden' or the shops instead of finding out what I had to do with my scooter. They came back hot and flustered.

'The place wasn't close by at all, and there was a long wait in the queue. I thought the woman in front of me would never stop asking questions,' said Sue, sounding frustrated. 'But the person serving was very helpful and rang lots of places. There's somewhere about half an hour away in a shopping centre. We'll need a taxi.'

Sue showed me the address—Underetagen, Hvidovre.

'Gee, how do you pronounce that? I'm pleased it's written.'

We caught a taxi, putting the collapsed scooter in the boot.

'That's where the first brewery was,' the taxi driver told us as we went past a large block of old buildings with some construction work going on.

'I've been there, years ago,' said Sue. 'We went on a tour with free beer at the end.'

'Yes, I can remember that too,' added Robin.

'It was Carlsberg Brewery, wasn't it?'

The taxi driver nodded in agreement.

It was interesting looking out at tall apartment blocks as we drove along, rather than the freestanding houses we see in Australian suburbs.

When I looked up the directions later, I saw we had gone about ten kilometres west of the Rådhus, through the Frederiksberg area, to Hvidovre.

'This is Rebæk Søpark centre here. What is the name of the place?' asked the taxi driver. Sue gave him the piece of paper.

'I can't see anything like that. Did they say where it was in the shopping centre?'

'No, sorry.'

'There's a phone number here. I'll try that,' said the taxi driver and called with his mobile phone. 'It's underground.'

He drove around to the back of the centre and into an entrance leading underground. We went down into a dark space with concrete walls, like a small bunker. There were three large motorbikes parked in a corner of the bunker. We all just sat there in the taxi, looking and not knowing what to do.

The taxi driver pointed to an exit near the motorbikes. Sue got out and went to investigate, coming back with a man in overalls and, yes, it was the right place. They took the scooter out of the boot and I paid the taxi driver with a tip and a big thank you.

We went through the opening into an area where there were dozens of motorbikes sitting in an open workshop with two mechanics working on various bits and pieces hanging down from the ceiling.

There weren't any mobility scooters, wheelchairs or any disability products to be seen. My scooter was in the middle of a workshop with motorbikes, bike parts and other odd pieces of metal.

My yellow scooter in the workshop

We tried to explain what had happened, but our explanation wasn't good. The man who seemed in charge was genuinely interested in helping us, but his English wasn't good, and our Danish was non-existent. We didn't seem to be getting anywhere, and my scepticism about the place was increasing.

I asked if he had ever seen scooters like mine before—Luggie scooters. Yes, he had heard of them and asked how long we would be in Copenhagen.

'Until next Thursday.' We were flying out early next Friday morning to Kangerlussuaq in Greenland to board the ship. I'd been looking forward to the Greenland trip for so long. I had to have the scooter ready by then. And, besides, we had only been in Copenhagen a few days. There was more to do, and we were thinking of going to Sweden for a day and to Helsingor and to... My anxiety level was rising.

After thinking for a while, he said there was plenty of time and he should have a solution by then. He wanted me to leave the scooter there.

'But I need it to move about, to get anywhere.'

He offered me a rental scooter.

'Do you have any small ones like this one of mine?'

'No, sorry, bigger,' he said as he went away for a short while and came back driving a huge, big momma of a disability scooter similar to the ones we often see in Australia. I was incredibly surprised. I didn't expect to see such a vehicle in a motorcycle workshop, and it was huge.

'Heavens, that's big.'

He had nothing smaller and left again to get the charger.

'But how do I get this back to the hotel? We are a long way away and it won't fit into the boot of a taxi.'

'The train. The Metro, just over there.'

The Metro! I'd never been on a train or a Metro with such a huge vehicle. I didn't think I would know how to manage, drive or ride on it. I hadn't used the local train system with my little scooter, let alone this giant one. I must have looked lost because the man quickly told me to get on and practise before I left.

I hopped on and it wasn't difficult. It was the same as the one I'd tried a few years ago when I was testing scooters for the first time. So, I had ridden a big one. But I still had trouble believing that I had to leave my scooter behind. I didn't want to go on the train with the big scooter. I wanted my little one.

'But how do I get to the Metro? How do I get on the train? And where do we get off? Do we have to change trains?'

The man told us Rødovre station was just on the other side of the road from the shopping centre, with a ramp over the road and an elevator on the other side. He said they had people coming there on their mobility scooters all the time.

'There are more mobility scooters and wheelchairs in a room out the back. There's too many of them to fit in here.' It was a genuine place.

I realised that I'd have to leave my scooter and battery at this place and trust they'd look after it and try to fix it. He seemed like a nice man.

'Here is my name—Sulli, and my mobile phone number.' He handed me a piece of scrap paper. Sulli also said sorry, but he had to charge US$50 a day for the rental and asked for the name and number of our hotel.

I left him the details and was preparing to leave when Sulli let us know that the trains leaving Rødovre station, going to the city, all stopped in Østerport near our hotel. We wouldn't have to change trains.

'Thank you. Great. And how long will the charge last?'

Two or three days was his answer, but he wanted to check the large scooter again before we left because they hadn't charged it for a while. Sulli checked the battery indicator level on the scooter and then plugged the charger in, asking one of the other mechanics if the correct lights came on.

The younger mechanic looked quickly, hesitated and then replied, nodding, 'Ja, okay.'

Sulli gave us the charger in case we needed it.

We took the bag off the back of my scooter with the flat, old battery in it, leaving the other one in the scooter. I gave Sulli my email address, and we left to find our way back to the hotel.

The big scooter went up the steep exit from the bunker easily, and I was surprised at the power it had. Outside the centre, we went across to the far corner to some bushes where we found a ramp. The big scooter moved swiftly, and I didn't feel any bumps. It was comfortable and I just about flew along, leaving Sue and Robin way behind.

There was a large lift on the other side of the ramp, and we went down to the station ticket office. I was impressed with the accessibility of the place. Sue purchased three tickets and checked the time of the next train. It was in a few minutes.

'Just sit out on the platform on your scooter, behind the line, and wave when the train comes in,' were my instructions from the ticket office.

I waved, and when the train stopped, I was outside the wrong carriage. The train driver came down and called us up closer to the front, to the carriage with bicycles and wheelchairs painted on the side that I had missed completely.

As the train driver put the ramp down, he asked, 'Where do you want to get off?'

'Østerport.'

'Where?'

'Østerport,' I said again. My pronunciation was terrible.

'Oh, yes,' he said, 'Ooo-sterport.'

My 'O' pronounced 'Oh' and I realised it should have been 'Ooo'. He said he would phone the station and ask them to have someone to meet us there with a ramp. 'Just wait in the carriage until someone arrives.'

What great service, I thought. I thanked him and rode the scooter up onto the train. The carriage had a few people sitting, but it was packed full of bicycles lined up at right angles. It was hard manoeuvring my big scooter around to a free area. But I made it and have a photo to prove it. I didn't run over or bump into anything. Me on Big Momma Scooter parked ourselves perfectly inside the carriage.

Me on Big Momma scooter on the train

A man with a ramp met us at Østerport station. It was easy getting off and he showed us the way to the lifts.

What a day we'd had. We bought some groceries at the supermarket just outside the railway station before heading home. Luckily, the supermarket also sold wine. We all needed a drink.

Back at the hotel, I made it through the front doors, then into the large-enough lift and went up to our floor. But in the corridor, the scooter was too big to turn. I saw a vacant spot in one corner of the hall with a power point. A perfect place to leave it to charge overnight.

Later, I highlighted where we'd walked that day on my map and read that the changing of the guard ceremony at Amalienborg Palace took place every day at noon. We all thought we'd try to make it the next day.

Apart from the one hot sunny day, summer in Copenhagen had not been warm. We had to wear layers of clothes, with temperatures of about 12°C. I had to have even more on to keep me warm riding the scooter. All rugged up, we set off the next day.

The gardens and parks in Copenhagen were a real joy. It surprised me to find so many within the city. We'd visited Kings Gardens and the Botanical Garden on my own scooter, going past Ørsted Park. Its paths looked more difficult. I thought now I had the bigger scooter it might handle them better.

We wandered through Ørsted park easily with Big Momma and took our time. Some paths were very steep, with loose gravel. My small scooter would have had trouble. It was a walking park with bushy and forested areas around two lakes, with occasional grassy areas for a picnic. Big Momma was ideal.

After we left, it thrilled us to see Queen Margrethe going past in a car guarded by police, leaving a parade at the Royal Guards' base. But the changing of the guard ceremony at the palace would have to wait for another day.

When we finally arrived near the palace, it was late afternoon. The Marble Church, just up from the palace, with its stunning huge green dome, was still open. We stopped at the pedestrian crossing in front of it, ready to cross quickly.

But my big scooter only made it halfway across the road and stopped. Sue and Robin came running back.

'Oh no! What's wrong?'

Because the cars were all about to move, I quickly got off and found the brake lever and released it so we could freewheel the scooter back onto the footpath.

I got back on the scooter and tried to get it to move, but nothing happened. We all agreed the battery was flat and needed re-charging.

Thankfully, we'd brought the charging unit with us in the basket. It just had to be connected to a power point. We were at the northern end of the old city of Copenhagen, with more historical buildings or businesses than the cafés that had proven to be good sources of power points in the past.

Sue spotted a café down the road and went off to investigate. Robin and I pushed the scooter over to the street corner.

The Marble Church (or Marmorkirken) was an impressive church sitting straight in front of us. It has been called 'one of Copenhagen's most imposing architectural assets.' St Peter's in Rome inspired the dome. The building style is neo-baroque and rococo. Combined with the dome, it makes a grand landmark.

I was in an area called Frederiksstaden. The palace, the opera house, and the church are positioned elegantly in a line. Amalienborg Palace has several wings, for different groups of the royal family, spread out around open public space. Behind it, across the water, the modern national opera house stands out with its equally impressive and different 'neo-futuristic' style. Everything around me seemed to be named Frederik-something, named after King Frederik, who founded the new quarter in the mid-1700s. The street I was standing on was even called Frederiksgade. The other name for the Marble Church is also, unsurprisingly, Frederik's Church.

Sue came back saying, 'No, they are closing in a few minutes. But they recommended Oscar's up the road the other way. They're open until late at night, apparently.'

Oscar's looked good—a bar, café and restaurant on a corner near a small square. Sue went inside to ask if we could use a power point.

'Yes, come in. No problem at all,' said one of the staff coming out with Sue.

'What about the scooter?' I asked.

'Oh, yes, please bring it in too. There's plenty of room,' she said. 'I'll show you where the power points are. My name is Olivia.'

The three of us pushed the scooter in and Olivia showed us to a spare table at one side, where she moved a few chairs out of the way. We took our jackets off and settled in for a few hours of charging. We plugged the scooter charger in, but no charging light came on.

'Is this power point working?' I asked.

'It should be. Let me try my mobile and charger with it,' suggested Olivia. She plugged it in. 'Yes, it works; see how my phone lights up.'

'That's strange,' I said. 'But can we try our charger on another power point, anyway?'

Sue went with Olivia and the scooter charger into another room. When they came back, they said it wasn't working. Come to think of it, I didn't notice if a light came on when I plugged it in at the hotel.

We had a big momma of a scooter that was going nowhere, and we had no way to charge it. We all looked blank for a while. 'Let's just sit down and have a drink and think about what we're going to do,' suggested Sue. 'I'm having a beer. Anyone else?'

'Yes, why not, looks like we'll be here for a while,' I answered.

'I think I might even have one,' said Rob. 'It's been years since I had a beer.'

The three of us settled in at the table while Olivia went off to get our beers.

'We'll have to ring Sulli and ask him what to do,' I said. 'I know it is late on a Saturday, but what else can we do? He gave me his mobile phone number.' I looked through my handbag for the piece of paper with his number but couldn't find it.

Then I remembered. I left it back in the hotel room. 'Let's ring the hotel and ask if someone could go up to our room and get the number for us,' Sue suggested. 'I'll ask Olivia if she'll let us use their phone. What's the hotel number?'

Using Olivia's mobile phone, Sue called the hotel and nicely (Sue was good on the phone) pleaded for help. Then she turned to me, 'Where exactly is that piece of paper with Sulli's name on it again?'

I told her I thought it was on the coffee table, under the tourist guide.

'What's the number they can ring us back on?' asked Sue walking over to Olivia, who wrote the number down. Someone at the hotel was going to look and ring back.

We waited with Olivia's phone and had a few more sips of beer. We each had a different sort–a Carlsberg, a Tuborg and, appropriately, as we were near the place, a Royal, and agreed they were all good.

We didn't have to wait long for a call back from the hotel with the number. By this time, it was about 6pm on a Saturday and I didn't really expect Sulli to answer, but I rang, hoping he would.

'Ya...' he answered straightaway. I told him about the problems we had with their scooter and charger. He said he had wondered about the old charger. Then he surprised me by saying he thought he had fixed my scooter (after only one day) and asked where we were.

'Café Oscar.' He knew where it was and asked if we could wait there for one to two hours.

'Yes, sure.'

He said he would get someone to bring my scooter to us and asked if I could pay in cash. Yes, I was carrying enough.

We could hardly believe it. I was getting my scooter back. Olivia was happy for us to stay.

Everyone working at Oscar's was friendly and chatted to us from the bar or when they went past. The whole place had a relaxed atmosphere, and it was warm inside out of the cold. We just made ourselves even more comfortable and ordered more drinks.

People were sitting outside on the pavement at cane tables and chairs, happily drinking, eating and talking. The traffic going along the street thinned and went more slowly as the evening progressed.

When we offered to pay for the phone calls, Olivia refused our offer. More customers came in more often, and Olivia had to go back and stay behind the bar. Things were getting busier.

We sat and waited. Sue loved telling stories of happily driving around various countries in Europe with friends for months and the things that happened. Sometimes finding other friends without any proper directions or location. They just found each other in whatever town or city the other person said they'd be at on an approximate date. And they were there, and they did meet up. No mobile phones needed. Sue has never forgotten one particular event.

'I remember when you and I were in Spain, Rob, and we suddenly realised we had to drive to Denmark and be there in two days. I don't know how we did it, but we were there in time for you to enrol in that course.'

An hour and a half had passed, when a tall man in khaki overalls came in, looked around and came straight up. Yes, we were the ones with the scooter. He disappeared and then reappeared, pulling my scooter. It was wonderful seeing it.

He showed me how the power came on and handed me the bill. I invited him to sit down, but he said he didn't have time and had to go to another job, so I paid him.

'What will we do with the big scooter?'

'I will take it.' He left, pushing the big scooter out.

As much as I wanted to see how they fixed my scooter, I wasn't going to take the battery out and look. The main thing was it worked.

'Let's go.'

'It's darker now,' noted Sue. 'Do you have enough battery charge to get it all the way home?'

'Oh, I can see that the battery level is in the middle. Sulli did say they didn't have time to fully charge it. It may not last. Let's get a taxi.' Everyone agreed with my taxi suggestion for once.

From the footpath outside, I saw the man in khaki overalls across the road, pushing the big scooter up into the back of a van. Incredible service, I thought.

Back at the hotel, we thanked the reception staff. I excitedly told them the whole story and Sue had to stop me because she could see I had lost them somewhere along the way.

Up in our apartment, I plugged my scooter in to charge and it started. I still didn't want to look closer at the work Sulli had done. It was time for dinner and a glass of wine.

After dinner, and with the battery fully charged, I took it out and noticed a new piece attached. The compartment at the base didn't look any different. I put the battery back in and checked that the red light still came on.

'Look at this. What do you think is happening?' I said, most surprised. Sulli's team had glued and screwed a short piece of rubber onto the battery to make it connect.

'I thought they would have fixed the part on the scooter, not do something to the battery.'

'Well, it works,' said Sue.

'Yes, but what about the other battery?'

'Let's put it in and see.'

I put the other flat one in, and it seemed to charge with no problem. 'It seems to be connecting all right. Let's see what happens in the morning.' It had been a long day.

Next morning, the older battery was fully charged and working. That's odd, I thought. When I took it out, nothing was holding it in place to connect. It didn't need a clip or an extra piece of rubber. I sat on the floor, looking at the batteries and thinking.

The older battery was slightly larger—that's why it was connecting—but now it came out too easily. I could see it jumping out whenever we went over a bump. Then I remembered that was why they changed the Velcro straps to the firm clip.

'Can you pass me that little booklet and some of those papers, please, Sue? We've got two of those black straps we put around the scooter at the airport, haven't we? Can you get one, please?'

I arranged the booklet, rolled papers on top of the battery, wound the black strap under the scooter base and back over the top of my weight, and pulled it down firmly.

'There, that should hold it. The plastic piece that broke off held the battery firmly in place, didn't it?'

'Yes, a bit too strong.'

'I think we should put the weight on the other battery too. That new rubber piece doesn't hold it in enough.'

With the new battery arrangements, we continued exploring Copenhagen.

The changing of the guard ceremony involved serious marching, and we had to keep well behind the safety line as the Danish Royal Guard came past and almost walked straight over us. They had uniforms of sky-blue pants with long, white stripes; dark-blue tunics with white straps, crossed at the front, and unusual furry headgear made of bearskin.

I'd heard about Christiania before arriving in Copenhagen. It was supposed to be different—an alternative community of modern hippies. But when we went there, it was weird. The alternate living I saw was housing falling down in a dirty area with lots of alcohol being consumed and who knows what else, as people collected in small groups, looking like they were doing deals.

It frightened me at times, and I wished I had the big momma scooter to get through there more quickly and with some protection. All eyes were on my yellow scooter and I felt they were keen to get it out from under me. We were glad to leave.

Nearby, Experimentarium City had a sunny waterfront area with a food market within a large tin shed. Comfy deck chairs were everywhere on the water's edge. We grabbed some spare ones and sat looking at the canal with ferries passing by, and over to the city area where the Royal Danish Playhouse, with its prominent glass-encased top storey, stood out. People were sitting out there too.

On our way around Copenhagen, we noticed young people standing up partying on open-backed trucks with loud music playing and horns honking. They all wore white caps that looked like ship captains' hats. The caps had coloured bands, and there were different colours worn on different trucks. I asked locals what was happening. They told us about the Danish tradition of celebrating with graduation caps, every June, when high school students finish their final exams. We saw people walking around or sitting in cafés and bars wearing the caps too. I hadn't seen people wearing those before. Apparently, they are specific to the school, with writing and markings inside showing misadventures, achievements or good wishes. Some students keep wearing their caps for most of summer and save them as graduating mementos. We wrote on our school shirts on the last day I was at high school and I still have mine.

Several people stopped me and asked about my scooter. They thought I was a local and wanted to get one. They had not seen one so small. I gave them the Luggie details and let Sulli know in case he wanted to stock some.

Having learned how and where to wave at the train driver for assistance, we went out of Copenhagen by train to Malmo in Sweden, over the Oresund Strait, imaging the Scandi noir TV drama *The Bridge*. Another day, we caught the train to Helsingor, site of Kronborg Slot or Elsinore Castle in Shakespeare's *Hamlet*. I really got the hang of train-waving during our stay.

After seeing Robin off, we flew the next day to Kangerlussuaq, Greenland, to join the expedition cruise. The scooter went well with my makeshift device, going over the ship, into polar circle boats, up and down ramps and bumps, including Greenland's uneven roads.

I saw a lot more of Copenhagen than I expected and also had my first experience of a large mobility scooter in a foreign place. On old cobblestoned streets, it was much more comfortable. The big scooter was faster, and the fully charged battery would last a lot longer than the one on my scooter. I can understand why they are so popular.

They fitted a new clip when we got home, with instructions to push it in before putting the battery in and also before taking it out.

'Don't just pull the battery up.' Yes, logical.

I think too much sometimes, but it occurred to me that if we had started the day in Copenhagen with the new, smaller battery in place when the clip broke, the charged old, larger battery replacing it would have worked, and with a weight on top things would have worked out. We could have got by with one battery.

But then we would never have gone to the bike shop, never seen that part of Copenhagen, never tried Big Momma, wouldn't know to wave to the train driver to get assistance, would not have gone to the park and would never have sat in friendly Oscar's.

5. THE GREENLANDIC PEOPLE (2015)

There was something about the Greenlandic people that struck a chord. An inner uniqueness that I considered must be because of both genetics and learning. Their minds and bodies seemed to have developed in a special way.

I wouldn't use the word 'supernatural', but whatever it was, it was something only natural to a Greenlander. That was the feeling I got early in our visit to Greenland, and it kept coming back throughout the trip.

On our cruise to the west Greenland coastline, we were lucky to have Greenlandic people with us as part of the expedition team. They were born and bred in Greenland or immigrants who wanted to live there. They explained and showed us their fascinating culture.

Greenlanders have an incredible sense about their environment and all aspects of it–the weather, the conditions, the wildlife, the materials available and their fellow people. They've learnt to survive and adapt to the most severe of conditions and events. They could feel the earth beneath and around them. They knew things before they happened. They dealt with grievances very differently. Their culture felt unique and admirable.

Out of Greenland's population of around 57,000, eighty-eight percent are from Greenlandic Inuit descent. The other twelve percent are mostly Danish.

Greenland is large, almost the same size as the whole of the eastern side of Australia, eighty percent of which is covered with a predominantly flat ice sheet.

The coastal areas, many that are mountainous, are mostly icecap free and green in summer.

Most people live in towns on the warmer western side of the island where we were. Sixteen-thousand people, nearly a quarter of Greenland's population, live in Nuuk, the capital.

Lying between Scandinavian Europe and Canada, Greenland's history has connections to both these areas. The Inuit peoples from nearby Northern Canada first moved there in 4500 BC. The Vikings from the east arrived later in the 10th century.

Most of Greenland lies above the Arctic Circle. Oodaaq in the country's far northeast is only 700 kilometres from the North Pole. It is thought to be the most northern landmass in the world, even though it is only a bank of gravel that seems to appear and disappear.

We flew from Denmark over the ice cap to the western town of Kangerlussuaq, inland from the Davis Strait in a fjord. Located midway up the west coast of Greenland, it was once used as a US military base.

After we landed, we travelled by bus for about an hour and a half to visit the edge of the ice cap.

Along the way, we passed beige coloured sand and sand hills which we stopped to look at. I couldn't believe what I saw. I expected rock or permafrost, but it looked more like a tropical island scene. But it could never be-the average summer temperature here was only 5 to 10 degrees Celsius.

The edge of the ice cap was a wonder to behold. An immense mass of thick ice rising that seemed to spread out forever. A few icebergs dropped off into lakes and the odd waterfall ran down like a glacier, except the extent of this beast was enormous. It covers 1.7 million square kilometres.

Edge of the icecap in Greenland

We didn't see any people or settlements on the way to the icecap. Just land and ice, then more ice. When we arrived back at Kangerlussuaq, the polar circle boats were waiting at a tiny pier to take us to our ship.

The next ten days we sailed down the west coast of Greenland. We visited towns with me scootering over their bitumen roads and gravel edges, glided in small boats amongst icy glacial deposits and carvings, spoke with locals and listened to talks.

Greenlandic people have strong cultural practices and beliefs. They're serious about fairness, respect, and the value of the land and creatures around them. They hunt only enough for themselves and to share. Greenland was built on these principles. Now they are a modern fishing nation, but still follow the same traditions, so there is always enough left.

Our Greenlandic expedition team members were passionate about their country, both its past and present. Two were born and raised in Greenland and had studied at the country's business school in Qaqortoq.

There was something unique in their culture that had survived. Their music, clothing, language, myths, food and homes are all alive with customs and tradition.

They treated us to a drum dance one night on the ship. One of the dances showed how disputes might be settled. It was a real-life lesson.

Each person's story was explained to those around them, as they spoke, danced and beat the drum. They wore traditional dress with painted faces of various meanings. It was a different way to hold some sort of mediation process or court of law session. More considerate and kindly. The role of the drum was something special too. And I heard the word 'magic' used more than once.

I came to realise one would have to spend a long time learning all their customs, traditions and beliefs to understand.

At some stages I wasn't sure if I was imagining what this special feeling was or whether I just wanted to have it, in some, for the want of a better word, 'romantic' way. I wanted it to be true, because the whole idea of human beings having such a sense really appealed to me.

They seemed such good people too. They didn't take more than they needed, and they shared what they had amongst each other. They lived in communities and worked together. They lead a simple life in one way, but an extremely difficult one. Adapting, surviving and managing the harsh environment.

I'll always remember a question from a fellow passenger after a talk one day. He was an older man with an American accent,

'But how do you make money?' I think he might have missed the point.

Access to the sea is critical to Greenlandic life. The country's four small cities, eighteen towns and 120 villages are all on the coast or on islands.

The sea had a lot going for it. One good thing was the absence of mosquitoes when we were at sea!

I had read and seen photographs of people in Greenland madly waving their hands in the air to brush the creatures away. On shore, the mosquitoes were always there, but their intensity grew when we travelled south.

At the beginning of the trip, no one wore netting over their faces, but the numbers of visiting passengers wearing netting increased the further south we were. At one town, even the locals wore netting. I had hefty insect repellent on my head, but my hands never stopped moving.

'What other little creatures are there in Greenland?' Sue wondered out loud.

'There's a section here on my big map of Greenland, under 'wildlife',' I said as I showed it to her.

It listed plants, reindeer, muskox, Arctic fox, Arctic hare, collared lemming, polar bear, walrus, ringed seal, whales, narwhal, geese, ptarmigan, waders, snow bunting birds, auks, sunny owl, eiders, gyrfalcon and butterflies.

We'd also learned of other animals living there–sheep and dogs. Mosquitoes weren't mentioned.

We only saw one muskox the first day we arrived, near Kangerlussuaq, but we were going to berth near Grønnedal soon where we were told entire herds could be seen grazing. We wouldn't be seeing any polar bears as they were further north from where we were.

I later read the ancestors of the Greenlanders originally came from central Asia and spread eastwards. They crossed the Bering Strait between Russia and Alaska and moved across the north of Canada. It was only a short trip then by boat or sledge across to Greenland.

When we reached Paamiut, we visited the museum. The young woman looking after it told us she came from Denmark and had married a Greenlander. They lived in Paamiut, a small town with about 1,500 inhabitants. She had learnt a lot about the place and the country and was very proud of it all.

'Where are all the people?' I asked her. We had not seen very many at all walking, or around the town when we wandered around.

'They're out hunting. Most of the time they go out fishing, but in the last few days they've gone out in their boats to look for muskox. You can often see them grazing on land from the sea. Then our people go on to the land and hunt on foot.' We chatted with her for a little while and then had a look inside the small museum. The traditional clothes in glass cabinets were amazing. Such bright colours, all made from very different materials, like parts of animals and fish.

Later on the trip, we visited the main museum, the Greenland National Museum and Archives, in Nuuk. Fresh posters lined one wall. The Arctic Winter Games were going to be held there in 2016. The last games in 2014 were held in Fairbanks, Alaska.

The Arctic Winter Games is an international biennial celebration of 'circumpolar sports and culture' that involves regions and territories within seven countries that lie closest to the North Pole. Judging from the photos and posters, it is a very popular event. Many were wearing traditional costume, some still very appropriate for the activities and conditions.

The games are organised to raise awareness of cultural diversity and there is a focus on fair play in the competitions. It is both a cultural and sporting event where different Arctic peoples can learn more about each other.

The events included four skiing sports, two racquet sports, and nine Arctic sports. Ones I'd never heard of were 'Primitive Biathlon' and 'Dene Games', something else to look up when I got home.

The national museum also houses the famous Qilakitsoq mummies. The mummies, the bodies of three women and a child of six-months were discovered in Qilakitsoq, Greenland in 1972. The remains date back to 1475 AD.

There is a university in Nuuk and also cultural and research institutions. It seemed like a busy small modern city.

In a few of the other places, we saw several houses that didn't look well cared for. While wandering through one of these towns, I came across an older man who was intoxicated and walking back home with more bottles in his bag.

Another American man I met on the trip said he had visited Greenland twice before. He told me he had been to the east coast where there was a high alcohol problem. That side of the country is much more remote and being cut off from the rest of Greenland was not doing as well as the west coast. But even the west coast seemed to have an occasional problem too.

When I was back home in Melbourne, I learned more about the Greenlandic people. I went to see a plastic surgeon for surgery on a skin cancer. While I was there, I told him I'd just come back from Greenland and there was something special about the people there. He seemed to understand straight away.

'You'll have to read a great book I know that says something about the people. It's called *Miss Smilla's Feeling for Snow*. It's a sort of a murder and detective story, but that's more the story line to really talk about Danish and Greenlandic people. It's set in Copenhagen and it's very interesting. I'm sure you'll like it,' he said.

I later read the book and really enjoyed it. It confirmed some special attributes that I believed Greenlandic people had.

To name one was the way Smilla could feel snow, interpret how it fell and the way it lay.

She could also feel ice under her feet and how thick it was. Walking and running over it, adapting her body to the ground saved her life more than once. When she put her traditional boots on, she could feel even more. I instantly recalled the traditional clothing I'd seen in the museum in Paamiut, especially the boots.

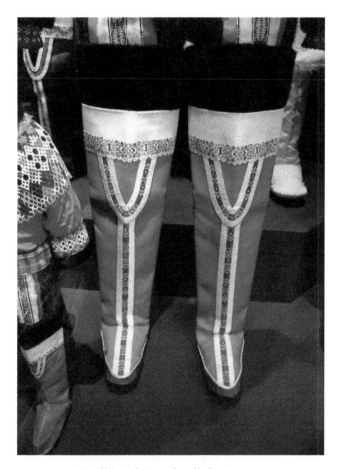

Traditional Greenlandic boots

The boots looked amazing, but I wondered at the time how anyone could walk in them. I wish I'd tried a pair on. Then I might have had a better insight into that special connection Greenlandic people had with the land and environment. I might have even walked better! It all seemed amazing. Magic.

6. VENICE AIRPORT (2015)

There was one front wheel missing when the airport attendant brought my scooter out at the Venice Marco Polo Airport. For the last five years, and when we left Amsterdam, there were two wheels close together at the front. Now there was only one.

My mobility scooter had been going well, with only minor mishaps in its life so far. But at the airport in Venice there was another new tale evolving. I'll go back a few steps first.

On the day we landed, it was chaotic. We were asked to wait in the middle of a disorderly crowd with our bag and me in an airline wheelchair while the attendant assisting me went to get my scooter from whatever baggage area it had arrived. The young man wheeled my collapsed scooter along to us, and Sue noticed something first.

'Where is the other front wheel?' she asked, pointing to the missing wheel area.

'Oh, it still goes along. Look, it will be fine. It will be all right, see it still moves,' the young man said, in a smooth Italian accent. He didn't seem to understand.

'No, I don't think so,' I quickly jumped in. 'It will topple over. It won't last long. Look, it will fall over as soon as it goes over something uneven,' I responded, rocking the scooter to demonstrate.

'Do you think you could go back and see if you can find the other wheel? It might still be in there where it fell off,' Sue insisted. The fellow went off and came back in a few minutes with a small wheel in his hand.

'See it goes on here,' I showed him. 'It's an important part!'

'I will report the damage. But that will take time. And they won't fix it here.'

'Yes, alright, but we need some record of this before we leave.'

We had a few hours to spare before we were due to check in on the ship. We had time. But then we also had a pickup booked that was waiting (hopefully). We would have to get a message out to them so they'd wait. It could be a bus or a car. I wasn't sure. Apparently, it all depended on how many people requested a transfer to the ship from the airport.

Just meet in the arrivals area and there will be someone holding a sign, the email said. I thought it wouldn't take long to report what had happened to my scooter. How we'd get the scooter fixed–I'd worry about that later. Let's get it recorded and get to the ship before it leaves.

The situation in front of the lost and damaged baggage section was a worse chaotic mess, with no lines of queuing and tempers fraying everywhere. Some people were speaking loudly or shouting, others were gesticulating wildly, and a poor man with a walking stick was pushing his wife in a wheelchair and trying to push a large bag that was damaged at the same time.

It seemed like a constant flow of people straight from the baggage collection area to the counter. Everyone's baggage seemed to have had something happen to it.

At two glass sliding windows above the counter at the front of the crowd there was a sign *Lost and Found* written under Italian-looking words over the top. It was right beside the baggage collection area, almost as if most baggage was guaranteed to end up there.

Our young man left us and tried to bypass the sort of line with no luck. He tried the next sliding window opening. No luck. He came back to us now and then and kept trying to get some attention.

When he came back, I asked, 'Can we somehow get a message to the people outside, waiting to pick us up, to let them know we're still here?'

'If you go out, you will not be allowed back in here again.' Neither Sue nor I could go. We needed to stick together. I would not have been able to manage on my own. We just had to hope they'd wait.

While we were waiting, I took a few photos of the detached wheel and the scooter at the front to show where it had fallen off.

One of the two front scooter wheels missing

I thought they might come in handy as evidence. It could've been almost an hour, and we were getting nowhere. In the middle of our wait, our young man said he had to leave and attend to other passengers. He said he'd phoned someone, and they would come and meet us to help.

'Sure.' What else could we say? We waited a bit longer. I tried riding the scooter a little to check it'd move forward. I was careful and moved the weight of my body slightly over to the side where there was a wheel. If I went slowly, it was okay. We had already checked the outside of the scooter for signs of any other damage, and there wasn't any.

Someone came with a piece of paper with the phone number written down for us to ring to report what had happened. That would have to do, we thought. I'd had time to think about what we'd do after we left the airport.

'Let's just leave and get to the ship. We'll work out what to do from there.'

Sue said, 'They've probably had problems like this before on the ship. They should be able to help us. Yes, let's go.' The crowd at the counters hadn't changed much.

There must have been some security about, but it seemed to be a free-flowing exit into the arrivals area. I don't recall seeing anyone check on us.

I'd toyed with the idea of booking a water taxi to the ship from the airport. That sounded like an exciting way to go. In the end, I thought it may be more difficult for me, as lovely as it sounded. I'll go for the easy option—taxi (or it might be a bus).

'I hope someone's still waiting.'

In the arrivals area, there was a man in a black suit and sunglasses with a sign and our names written on it. I just about kissed him! 'Oh, thank you for waiting. I'm so sorry we've kept you waiting. You wouldn't believe what happened in there!'

'Please, this way', the man indicated with his hand. We followed him to a very nice black Mercedes, shiny and clean. I talked to the man again, and then he said he couldn't speak much English.

Sue and the chauffeur fitted the scooter and our bag into the large boot. I got in the front. I said a few words to Sue, then there was silence. I was interested in looking around the new territory. I'd never been to the airport and didn't have a clear map in my mind of where it was in relation to the port or where the ship was supposed to be. But this was Venice again, thirty-eight years after I first arrived by bus. I looked about with interest at everything.

Somehow after a while I got the feeling we were not going where I thought we should be. Something must have twigged in the driver's mind too because he asked, 'Going to the Grand hotel?'

'No, we're going to the ship—the Queen Victoria. It is leaving today this afternoon.'

'Not the Grand hotel?'

'No.'

'There must be a mix-up.'

'Can you take us to the ship?' I begged from the front seat. Sue was sitting in the back, so hearing the conversation would have been difficult for her. She probably didn't hear anything and said nothing.

'Yes, we will go now', said the driver, turning the car in a different direction.

Oh good, I thought, remembering I'd booked an excursion in Venice leaving from the ship at 3pm before it sailed in the early evening. But we had to check in first. I hoped we'd make it.

We arrived at the port to check in, and I expected there to be thousands of people waiting to board. The Queen Victoria's capacity was about two thousand passengers. But there weren't many at all at check in, only a dozen or so. I didn't realise most people had embarked in Southampton at the beginning of a six-week cruise and were continuing on. Some others had joined in Barcelona or Rome. We were just booked on one two-week sector of the cruise from Venice to Istanbul.

As soon as we'd booked in and cleared security and customs, we asked one of the ship's crew where we could go for help with the scooter. They directed us to the purser's desk. There wouldn't have been enough time to get the scooter fixed in Venice. We had to get something organised fast because the Venetian Panorama excursion left at 3pm.

We headed for the purser's office. Almost there I came to a halt, struck by the beauty of the inside of the ship. By then we were in the grand lobby. Wow. I'd seen nothing like that on a ship before. Then again, I'd never been on such a luxury cruise ship. The grand sweeping staircase rose three levels, with balconies on each deck looking over it and a chandelier. The lush carpet, the fine wallpaper and carefully placed artworks were all elegant. A photo or two was definitely in order. There was time as the purser's office was close by.

The purser, in a sharp white uniform with epaulettes of rank on his shoulders, greeted us with a very proper English accent.

'How may I help you?'

I explained about the wheel that'd fallen off the scooter, still riding it with great care. Thank goodness we had the wheel, I thought to myself again.

'Let me see,' the purser said as he looked at the wheel and then came around to look at the scooter.

'Oh yes, that's a XX missing. We probably won't have exactly that part, but we should be able to find something to fit and put it back on again.'

'That would be wonderful, thank you,' I said gratefully.

'I'll get one of our wheelchairs so you can use that while you're waiting.' Wow, I felt so much better.

'We'll let you know when the scooter's ready and deliver it to your cabin.' The service was very impressive.

With me sitting in a wheelchair, we took off to the meeting place for our first excursion. Well, Sue pushed me, I mean. We disembarked down the ramp to the bus waiting to take us to the panoramic motor launch tour.

The boat was in another area of the port complex. On a map the port of Venice looks like it has piers, like fingers hanging down from a hand, where the hand could be the city of Venice itself.

The Grand Canal forms an S-shape as it traverses from the port through the city like a palmar age line. While the main train station of Stazione di Santa Lucia links closely into the port, some of its lines ride over the Canal Grande into the port. The whole port area is a collection of transport hubs where cars, trains, ships and boats meet.

At one stage when planning the trip, I thought we'd get the train from Amsterdam rather than fly because the station was so close. My scooter would've still had two front wheels too!

There were about thirty people on the motor launch as we went out into the Venetian lagoon or Laguna Veneta or just the laguna and past the modern residential area on the island of Sacca Fisola.

Part of the launch was open, and the sun was shining, still lovely and warm in October. Entering the Canale della Giudecca, with the island of Giudecca on our right, it wasn't long before we could see the Piazza San Marco or St Mark's Square in the distance to our left. The magnificent Basilica San Marco and its bell tower appeared out of the city near the water's edge. Postcards don't do it justice.

We kept our distance in the lagoon and progressed out further to motor past the islands of Murano, Burano and the cemetery island of Isola di San Michele.

The Italian guide spoke to us most of the way over his microphone, pointing out all the famous churches, movie stars' houses, hotels and other sights.

I must admit I couldn't understand most of what he was saying. His accent was heavily Italian, or perhaps he spoke the Venetian dialect. Not that I could tell the difference. But he seemed to speak so fast, the words came out as one long word lasting the duration of the tour. It was the first time I'd been out on the lagoon, and as lovely as the sound of the Italian language was, my mind went to the geography of where we were.

Venice is in the middle of an enclosed bay like a vast lake with so many other islands in it. I didn't know about the nature of the water surrounding the city until that day. Narrow entrances connect the Venetian Lagoon to the Adriatic Sea. A bridge connects Venice to the mainland carrying the road from the Marco Polo Airport to the port, railway station and Grand Canal.

We left the more open waters of the lagoon and headed back to the ship, passing much closer to St Mark's Square. The crowds in there were huge. So many people were trying to move over the Bridge of Sighs and take photos at the same time. No time to just stand and gaze (or sigh).

My memory of Venice was a fond one, of canal reflections of gondolas and houses in the still clear waters of the canals with few people about.

In a January winter of the late 1970s, I fell in love with Venice. It was and still is an unbelievable place. All that water lapping up against beautiful centuries-old buildings is like no other place on earth. Getting lost in small streets called Calle, Ruga, Salizzada, or Fondamenta was wonderful. I could stand and wonder then at the magnificent Doge's Palace with its connecting bridge to the old city dungeons with no concern of being jostled.

A few hours later, not long after we returned to the ship, the phone rang in the cabin and my scooter was fixed and ready. I could hardly believe it. The purser delivered it back to our cabin personally and took the wheelchair away. All fixed, no problems and no charge. Such service was incredible. The Cunard Line scored a big tick from me.

We were lucky enough to be sailing in 2015 when the '175 years of Cunard' were being celebrated. The three current 'Queen-ships'—Victoria, Mary 2 and Elizabeth, all sailed out from Southampton together in May to celebrate the formation of the Cunard Line and later the same month sailed together again up the Mersey River to Liverpool, commemorating the first transatlantic crossing. There were a lot of special events on our Queen's cruise to join in the celebrations.

All on board and with my scooter fixed, we were ready to sail with her too. Down the Dalmatian Coast to Zadar and Mum's favourite of Dubrovnik, on to Greek classics and Turkish marvels before disembarking in Istanbul.

I was able to use my scooter in those two weeks to go everywhere I wanted, even the cobbled, winding streets of Mykonos.

I just had to have my photograph taken beside the ship along the way.

Me on my scooter beside the Queen Victoria ship

When we were back in Melbourne, we took the scooter to Scooters Australia for a check-up on the wheel. They were very complimentary of the work done by the engineer on the Queen Victoria. Cunard has much to be recommended.

The whole cruise was an enormous success. Venice Airport was in the distant past.

7. SINGAPORE, THEN AND NOW (1980 AND 2016)

It was more than a year after my return when it hit me. Singapore had really changed. What I saw in 2016 bore little resemblance to what was there in 1980. It wasn't just that my memory needed refreshing. The place was different. When I was there at the end of the cruise, I found myself in an unrecognisable city that I'd made quite a few wrong assumptions about. The vast difference only gelled when I read a newspaper article and saw an Instagram post long after I got home.

It is astounding how Singapore has expanded so much, both horizontally and vertically. It has moved out and into the harbour through reclamation to an astonishing degree, and when that became unviable, the city nation's growth turned vertical with skyscrapers reaching up higher and higher. The once low-rise city spread its feet and raised its arms, becoming a towering megalopolis that is still going up. With limited options for the small island to grow, they have been so inventive. The Raffles Hotel now lies so far back from the waterfront that it was barely visible as we went past on the sightseeing bus. It wasn't just a few hundred metres back from the harbour's waterfront; it was now kilometres away.

In 1980, the old Chinatown was a busy ramshackle of wooden and tin buildings with narrow streets and people dressed in traditional clothes. I didn't remember seeing any footpaths, so I decided not to visit there with my mobility scooter. It was the wrong decision. When I later saw an Instagram post from a woman in a wheelchair on a paved laneway, it looked very accessible, nothing like what it was in the past. It would have been very possible for me to go there.

I don't have a diary to remind me of my visit in 1980, but I have photos. After all, that was one of the main reasons I went there–to buy a camera. There were lots of other reasons too, but back in those days it was the cheapest way to buy a good camera.

The photos I looked back at from my old album revealed only a little of what I remember. I was surprised. There were no scenes of the city, the harbour, the river, the architecture, the old Chinatown, the beach or gardens. They are the things I'd photograph now. The photos in my old album include some of a fruit market and of local people working there, a birthday cake on a hotel room table and the courtyard at the Raffles Hotel for dinner. Another set of photos has a series of round coloured lights in focus against a blurred background. I labelled those 'New Camera Testing'. There are some posed faces in other photos that I'd put in that same category now. Nothing to do with my age at the time, of course!

I was about to turn 27 years old on that trip. I would have been on annual leave from work at the hospital. For the first time I was earning a reasonable income, and I wanted to buy a good camera–a new Nikon SLR. I loved travelling, and it was one of a few good excuses to go to Singapore for a quick visit.

Another place I'll never forget from that trip was a nightclub I visited attached to a hotel. You wouldn't have guessed what it was like looking from the outside. When you went in, it opened up into an enormous, dimly lit space filled with dozens of Venetian gondolas surrounding a stage. The gondolas were arranged at different heights off the floor, each with a candlelit table and chairs in the middle. We sat in one, ordered drinks and watched the performances. One performance was a group of Asian people dressed in cowboy outfits singing American songs. I don't think it was karaoke, but who knows? It was in the early hours of the morning and we were having a good time.

On this latest trip, I'd booked to stay at the Marina Bay Sands Hotel, a new hotel on the reclaimed area just out of the city centre. It was its infinity pool at the top that I wanted to be in. I'd seen it in an advertisement sitting on top of a connecting link between two towers. It looked spectacular. I thought I'd be able to swim across to one side of the pool and look straight down over the edge across the city. What a great photo that'd make.

The pool looked exactly how it did in the advertisement, except it didn't show the masses of people in it. There was hardly any room for me to fit! Well, that's how I felt. Possibly with so many people I felt self-conscious walking with two sticks into the pool, or maybe I was just turned off at the sight. The people at the edge seemed to be having a good time, and it was a fantastic view.

I returned to the pool in the early evening, investigating the restaurants and bars also on that level. There were not as many people in the pool then, and I posed for a photo on my scooter beside it.

Me on my scooter at the infinity pool of Marina Bay Sands Hotel in Singapore

I assumed I'd be out and about around Singapore for about four to six hours every day before my scooter battery needed recharging. Sue and I were prepared. We had a new battery and an old spare one.

However, we had a problem with one battery because we struck a monsoon on the Thai island of Koh Samui, the last port of call before Singapore. There were '*unprecedented unseasonal monsoonal rains and flooding*' the headlines said.

When we were in Koh Samui, we took a half-day bus excursion. Sue and I were sitting up inside the bus and my scooter was in the luggage compartment underneath. The heavy rain started after about thirty minutes into the four-hour journey. The sheets of water running across the road rose higher and higher. Shops along the way had water flowing into them, and motorcycles and cars had their wheels covered. People were wading across the street with water up to their waists.

The flooded road in Koh Samui

The bus continued the tour over the flooded roads and most of the sights were impossible to see because of the torrential rain. Locals were out sandbagging, directing traffic around obstructions, and trying to protect their stalls along the roadside. We were riding high in the bus, looking about in amazement at what was happening. I didn't give any thought at all to my scooter below in the hold. At one stage, the bus caught some electrical wires hanging over the road and dragged them behind it for a while. The driver didn't stop. I was aghast.

Although the main sights weren't visible, it didn't seem to worry anyone on board. They were intent on looking at the scenes happening around us, taking turns to take photos and videos at the front beside the driver.

At the end of the tour, the bus dropped us back to the pier where we'd started. The rain had eased and the distance to the tender boat was only short, so I walked with my two walking sticks. Sue wheeled my scooter for me.

We had to use the local tender boats at that port because the ship wasn't allowed to use its own. It was probably something to do with following a rule and using local employment. I sat beside my scooter in the half-open boat. The floor was wet and there was more rain coming in.

Back on the ship, I rode my scooter to our cabin as it was too far to walk. It worked, then.

When we got back, we had to pack. The next day would be the last on our cruise. I didn't charge the scooter battery because I'd hardly used it. I left the scooter parked over in its usual spot in the room, tucked out of the way.

Come dinnertime, I hopped on the scooter to ride it to the dining room, but the light didn't come on and it wouldn't go.

'Something's wrong with the scooter,' I called out to Sue. I took the battery out and noticed there was water underneath it in the base. I wiped the base out and put the older spare battery in. I put the wet battery on some absorbent paper.

The scooter worked perfectly with the second battery in place, one I'd bought six years ago. For the last few years, the charge wasn't lasting as long as it used to, and I bought a new improved one with more power and longer life. The old one lasted up to about two hours in recent times, while the new one went for up to six hours.

After dinner, I checked the battery and found that the paper below was soaked. When I lifted the battery up water ran out.

'Oh no! Look what's happened here! It might dry out overnight. I think I'll just leave it here,' I said, after looking to see what the best way was to leave it to let any more water run out. At least we have the old one, I thought. We hadn't needed it on the trip so far. I charged it up for the following day in case the newer one still wasn't working.

Early next morning, water was still coming out of the battery when I lifted it up. We packed it away and left the ship, riding my scooter with the old one in place.

In Singapore, there was an ongoing saga with the wet battery for a short while until we gave up. We tried to get help from the hotel concierge. He contacted a disability supplier, but they were out in the suburbs and he didn't think they could help, anyway. We tried other methods to dry out the battery, but all failed. I just had to limit the distance I travelled on the scooter and return every one to two hours to the hotel for recharging. I carried the charger on the back of the scooter, just in case. We wanted to see Singapore.

The other reason for booking the Marina Bay Sands Hotel was its location right next to the new Gardens by the Bay development facing Singapore harbour. The new place had giant tree-like structures with walkways, but my attention went to the nearby cooled conservatories of the Flower Dome and the Cloud Forest. An electric public transport vehicle operated from the entrance to the park, stopping at various locations, and it had a space where wheelchairs or small scooters could fit. That saved travelling some distances and let me go around inside the two conservatories with less worry about the time.

The most impressive conservatory for me was the Cloud Forest. As well as the wonderful plants and trees contained under an enormous glass dome, there was a fabulous elevated accessible glass walkway. It took me up three floors, literally into the moist clouds, and it was perfect for me on my scooter. There was also a lift to different levels too.

Inside the Cloud Forest conservatory in Singapore

We had to be selective about other places we visited in Singapore and think differently about where we'd go. We caught the hop-on hop-off bus loading the scooter with the disability ramp. We stayed on and didn't get off. There were long queues at each stop, and we were afraid we might never get on again. It also whizzed along so fast, reconfirming to us why we rarely catch the hop-on hop-off buses. We see much more when we are walking.

Off the bus there was a great circular walk from the Marina Bay Sands shopping centre, across the road from the other side of the hotel, going around the newly created Marina Bay. Starting at the outstanding architecture of both the Art Science Museum, where one side looks like an opening flower and the Helix Bridge that is really a double helix, we walked on to The Float (a floating sports ground). Accessibility signs were everywhere as we continued around the bay to Merlion Park with the famous lion symbol of Singapore spouting water from its mouth. The Boat Quay behind the Merlion with its old buildings along the Singapore River was a great diversion with a fabulous spot to stop for a beer. Going back to the hotel, we passed another reminder of how different things were now. The old buildings and piers that were once harbour moorings have now been renovated and sit on the new inland bay. Looking around, I could see that a large area had been reclaimed and made more accessible. It was easy going on my scooter.

On another day we caught the small river cruise boat leaving from outside the Marina Bay Sands shopping centre and went up the Singapore River and back. The only problem was that the boat wasn't accessible. There was a ramp down, but nothing to get onto it. Sue had to take my scooter back to the ticket office. On board listening to the commentary, it was clear there had been massive changes and improvements everywhere. There were more things to see and do than I'd anticipated.

At the time, the temperature and humidity didn't seem to be too high for me either with my heat sensitive MS. I felt okay. I was surprised again when I read later that Singapore lies at only 1 degree north, almost on the Equator. I thought it should've been much hotter. But I could easily go back again.

I've got a list of more things to see next time, including the Botanic Gardens. Singapore is a new place for me, especially with my scooter. Next time, I'll go with no assumptions, in 'anything is possible' mode— and not go via a monsoon either!

8. FIRSTS BY CHANCE (2013 – 2016)

I've always wanted to see what First Class was like. I just needed a good reason to step over the divide. That happened after an email in 2013.

'Etihad are offering First Class seats for the price of Business Class,' friend Jane wrote. 'You said you always wanted to try Business Class one day. I thought it might interest you.'

My eyes popped wide open. This was an opportunity not to miss. I'd always booked Economy Class flights because I thought Business Class was an enormous expense that couldn't be worth it. I didn't want to spend that much money on just flying, even if it was for a long-haul flight. First Class I'd never considered.

I checked with Sue, and her eyes sprang open as wide as mine. She didn't think for long before she said, 'If Jane can do it, I suppose we can too.' Jane travelled with a friend in a wheelchair. They were ordinary people too. If not now, then when?

I booked the return First Class flights from Melbourne to Dusseldorf via Abu Dhabi.

The Etihad First Class flight experience was truly something else. When we arrived at our seats, I couldn't believe the compartment we'd each been given, with sliding doors to the aisles for privacy and buttons galore to press. We were in the two middle seats and could lower the screen between us to sit together, enclosed on all sides like one small room. And before we knew it, we were drinking vintage champagne served from a silver tray.

We were like children with new toys but trying to act grown up and look as if we flew that way all the time. The chef soon arrived to take our order. He asked us how we would like our food cooked and when we wanted it served. The cabin host brought different styles of sleepwear to choose. The amenities kits came in special cases with generous supplies of creams and perfumes, all well-known expensive French brands I'd never seen, let alone touched.

The quality and variety of the food and wine was outstanding. The wine list had Sue reading for ages, considering the vintages on offer.

When we wanted to sleep, the cabin crew came to help make our beds (Sue tried on her own and failed, I didn't know how) providing fluffy doona covers and heavenly pillows. Sleeping on the lie-flat beds was easy. I could lie down, move my legs, elevate my feet and sleep during the first nine-and-a-half-hour flight.

Mmm, this is how it's done. I suddenly understood.

Our night flight from Melbourne went directly to Abu Dhabi, where we would stay the night. I'd never been there but had read about a few sights to see, especially the new Sheikh Zayed Grand Mosque.

All was going exceptionally well until we were in the hotel room and told the onward flight the following day was no longer in First Class but Business Class.

Apparently, the First-Class seats in our booked aircraft needed some repair work. It wouldn't be ready until a day later.

I felt let down. I know we weren't paying the full First-Class fare, but that was not the point. I had never flown First Class, would probably never again, and I wanted to fly this time as I thought I was going to. I surprised myself by asking if they would compensate us for the change.

They told us we could still fly First Class but with Emirates airlines instead, on a flight out of Dubai. That was about 140 kilometres away.

'How would we get there?'

'We'll send a driver in a car to pick you up from your hotel in Abu Dhabi and take you to Dubai airport for the flight tomorrow morning. Would that be satisfactory?'

'Yes, thank you very much. It would.'

It was all arranged. We spent a day in Abu Dhabi that turned out to be only a few hours outside because it was so hot at over 40 degrees C. The hotel we were staying at arranged a taxi at a negotiated price to take us to the mosque and a few other places on my list. The mosque was a standout and a sight worth seeing. The other places were still being refurbished (such as the White Palace) or not open that day (the Women's Handicraft Centre).

When I got out of the air-conditioned taxi outside the Sheikh Zayed Grand Mosque, the hot air hit me again. But the sight of the more than grand, enormous white mosque with gold flourishes grabbed my attention. The clear blue sky made the white minarets and domes stand out as I hurried on my scooter to the entry.

The all-white complex covers 12 hectares of worship areas (for 41,000 people) surrounded by manicured green parks and gardens with large ponds of water. In a courtyard outside the main prayer hall, it was cooler as we tied on headscarves and placed our shoes on wooden shelves. Others were covering themselves completely in supplied black gowns, neck to ankle. Our dress of buttoned up long-sleeved blouses and long pants was acceptable. And unlike some other mosques, my scooter was allowed inside.

The light filled entry was covered everywhere in flower patterns— on tiled floors and walls, containing jewels, gems and ceramics. Garlands of flowers embroidered doorways and openings. Vines with flowers crept up the walls.

We moved into a reverently lit immense space with white marble pillars embedded with more flowers made from mother of pearl shells. Above the pillars the white and gold arches upon arches were covered in intricate floral patterns with complex fretted woodwork between arches higher up. The expansive ceiling had domes within domes covered in intricate light gold patterns, while small windows shaped as flowers were in some walls. A single piece of lawn green coloured carpet with pink flowers covered the entire floor. I was unsurprised later to learn that it is the largest hand-knotted carpet in the world. Also, the world's largest was a crystal chandelier weighing twelve tons in the shape of a flower hanging down, with more jewels for petals.

There were not many people inside the mosque the day we were there, leaving plenty of room to move in the 10,000-person space. A blend of modern Islamic architectural styles completed in 2007, it is an amazingly beautiful place.

Early next morning, our driver from the airline picked us up for the trip to Dubai. It was dark outside, but still hot. As we travelled on the motorway, I tried to engage the driver in some conversation, but he spoke very little. We passed an oil refinery that was brightly lit and saw the edge of the waters of the Persian Gulf on our left and the desert landscape to our right.

As we approached Dubai, I saw what appeared to be a rail line extremely high in the air. It really stood out. There were bubbles of what looked like stations up along the line too. I asked the driver what it was, and I thought he said the metro. It was very unusual. What a great idea, I thought. No need for a rail line anywhere near the ground, just build one up in the sky over the desert. I later read the Dubai Metro is a 'state-of-the-art, driverless, fully automated rail system that is clean, fast and efficient'.

We reached Dubai International Airport and I could see we were being delivered somewhere other than the usual airport entry area. There was no question, explanation or choice about any of it. It just happened. I'm not sure of the order of events, but my first recollection is being shown into a huge dining area with white linen tablecloths and silver service settings on dozens of tables with waiters in suits attending. There was hardly anyone else there. But it could have held hundreds of people. I thought it must have been the First-Class airport terminal restaurant area. I'd seen nothing like it at an airport before. I didn't realise so many people travelled First Class.

I parked my scooter nearby, and we sat down to eat with not just one waiter attending but several.

'Would you like freshly squeezed orange juice to start? How would you like your eggs cooked? Coffee? Espresso or...?' Breakfast was being served.

It was early in the morning and we'd been waiting to get to the airport lounge to have something before our flight. I knew about airport lounges from my experience with Qantas when I was working. So, I'd been to a few Business Class lounges before. But never First Class. That dining room was something else, with service and facilities such as I'd never seen or experienced anywhere. The meal was lovely and finished far too soon. I could have sat there a lot longer!

Someone came to take us to check-in for our flight. As I rode my scooter, my head was turning this way and that trying to take in the incredible surrounds as we moved from one area to another.

Things were going superbly, including with my mobility scooter. But there is often some drama with it along the way. The drama at Dubai airport came as soon as we arrived at the First-Class check-in desk.

'You can't take that,' the woman snapped.

'What do you mean? I need it.'

There was a kerfuffle, and we were asked to stand back off the line and wait. No one explained what was happening. It was still early in the morning and we'd been up for hours and I was beginning to feel tired. I lost my temper a little when a woman in a black hijab and long dress came over with a walkie-talkie to question us. She said it wasn't possible for my scooter to go on the plane.

I had to let Sue take over and try to keep quiet (at Sue's excellent suggestion).

The woman who I assumed was a supervisor told us, 'It might get damaged. We don't want to be held responsible.'

'But...'

'You'll have to wrap it up in protective plastic.'

'How?'

'You have to pay three Dirhams, about one Dollar for it to be done.' Heck, we are travelling First Class I immediately thought. Wouldn't you think they'd offer to do it anyway, for nothing? But it seemed some things are included, and some are not.

'That's ridiculous. I haven't got any change. I don't have any Dirhams left.' I ceased being quiet.

'It's about one dollar. Have you got any American Dollars?'

'I've got an Australian Dollar,' Sue jumped in. We are not paying anything, I thought, but didn't say. The supervisor explained again my scooter needed to be wrapped in special plastic.

'How will we do that?' I asked casually, really switched off by then.

'I can organise it to be done. I will call someone to collect the scooter.'

By then a wheelchair had arrived, and I sat in it.

'Oh, okay.' Sue gave the woman some money and wheeled me back to check-in as a man came to collect my scooter. Gee, I hope I see it again at the other end, I thought.

Armed with boarding passes, we made our way to security and the boarding gate. Then the next altercation took place.

'What's this?'

'The battery for my mobility scooter.'

'I'll have to get this checked. I don't think it's allowed. I'll have to call someone.'

Oh no, I thought. Not again. I got out my Material Safety Data Sheet and my Qantas airline approval and argued my case.

'I'll handle this,' Sue said. Good, I was being wheeled away for a body pat down, anyway. I left the paperwork with Sue. The security woman in a burqa and long black dress took me into a tiny room and pulled a curtain across the doorway.

After the search with few words spoken, and a little frightened, I emerged to see Sue with the battery.

'They didn't look at the paperwork,' she said, handing the sheets back to me. 'Another man came along, looked at the battery, turned it over and said okay!'

Once we boarded the aircraft, the mood changed immediately! It was a different world again. We were greeted with smiles and treated ever so nicely. Being in First Class was a bonus on the daytime Emirates flight. The cabin attendants had stylish middle eastern flourishes to their uniform, especially for the women's headgear, with silver trays of more vintage champagne appearing magically again like genies out of a bottle!

The seats had a dressing table on one side with mirrors that popped out. All the edging of the wood was gold, and I had a huge seat all to myself. Sue was in hers across the aisle just beside me. We were in a gold world with gold upon gold surrounding the seating. I must admit, it seemed a bit over the top. We didn't see anyone else in our cabin area.

We could have been in our own personal aircraft or gilded cage in heaven!

I can still remember my first snack that day—Russian blinis and black caviar with finely chopped egg pieces and a lemon wedge. They tasted superb. The flight was an easy six-hour daytime trip with no need for a lie-flat bed. The food and wine with movies on the entertainment screen were more than enough to keep us happy.

The scooter arrived safely in Dusseldorf, wrapped in so much plastic we needed cutting tools to remove it. But the scooter itself was undamaged.

On the return First Class flight with Etihad, it sounds funny, but I don't remember anything specific about it. I know we enjoyed being on the plane again, with the attention, the champagne and wine, the food, the lie-flat bed in our screened area. There were no hitches along the way. Getting off I walked out via the Business Class seats, ashamedly looking at the size of their area thinking to myself how well we did further up the front. We'd been spoiled. Thanks Jane!

On my first cruise ship experience on the SS Mariposa, our family stayed in a cabin with several bunk beds against the walls. There was little room in between to stand or move. I was 15 years old, and it was 1968. The seas were rough on that crossing and everyone was sick. We took turns vomiting into the toilet. There wasn't even a porthole in the cabin to look out of.

When I went later with friends on the Princess of Tasmania ferry in 1973, we sat up in lounge chairs to sleep, thinking it impossible to be able to pay for a bed.

In more recent years I'd been in better cabins with beds to sleep on, portholes or fixed windows. Being able to look out, to have a view, is something I love. The suites with large comfy beds and a private balcony were something only dreams were made of. Well, that's what I'd thought for well over thirty years.

The thing that helped me cross the line with ship cabins occurred a few years after the First-Class flight. I received the wrong mail in the post. It was a promotional flyer to someone else showing a special deal of free upgrades to balcony suites on the Queen Victoria ship with bonus cash to spend for early bookings. It jumped out at me. I recorded all the details before redirecting the mail to its rightful owner and went into action-booking mode.

Istanbul and the Black Sea were high on my to-do list. The cruise was from Venice to Istanbul with a circuit around the Black Sea stopping at some interesting places. I booked the cruise on Queen Victoria myself through the Cunard website.

Then in early 2015 Cunard notified me that the sectors of the cruise around the Black Sea had been cancelled because of the war in Ukraine. It wouldn't be safe. Alternative ports of call would be on Greek Islands and in Turkey. I could cancel our booking if I wanted to. Istanbul was still a big draw card and so was one other stop on the cruise, Dubrovnik. I kept the booking.

Later that year we were on the ship in a suite with a balcony. It had glass doors opening out from a large accessible room onto a private veranda. There was a ramp out of the cabin onto the balcony with plenty of veranda space to eat meals or have a drink. The weather from Venice to Istanbul in late September, early October in Europe was still very warm. The air conditioning inside the ship was great, but it was nice sitting out on the balcony.

In ports, the ship often moored right in the city and looking out from the balcony night or day was sensational. The view was there, available at any time. I didn't have to ride my scooter upstairs into one of the lounges with big windows to see the sights. I just had to go to one side of the cabin and either look out or go out onto the balcony. I will always remember sailing up the Bosporus and looking out over to the Blue Mosque, the Hagia Sophia and the Topkapi Palace in Istanbul. I understood and appreciated the difference between an inside cabin and a balcony suite. Another first.

In 2016, the following year, I was surprised when there was no other choice than First Class rail. We wanted to go from London to Berlin and chose to go by train. I wanted to go under the English Channel and see the European scenery at ground level, not from the air. The newish Eurostar train from London to Brussels fitted into the start of our trip perfectly. When I enquired about travelling using my mobility scooter,

Eurostar told me that the only disability seating was in First Class. And because I needed someone to travel with me, we would each only pay the Second-Class price to be in the First-Class carriage. Fantastic, I thought, yes!

The Eurostar train left London from St Pancras International. I knew it was a magnificent huge old building, especially from the outside, but the taxi dropped us off at the side entrance and the inside of the building was my view. However, it was difficult to see many features with the crowd. The tall marble columns supporting towering ceilings were impressive though.

Security was high, and we wove our way slowly to board the train. After assistance onto the First-Class carriage, I parked my scooter in a wheelchair space and sat on a comfortable, generous-sized seat with a table. There was plenty of leg room and a complimentary meal was served along the way. Tea and coffee were offered several times as the train sped quietly and smoothly along. We disappeared into one tunnel in England and saw light again in the French countryside. The whole trip was a joy.

Those were three incredible first experiences that I will never forget. I have never flown First Class again, but I have heard of train services where the only accessible areas are in First Class, so that might happen again. And I am always on the lookout for special cruise deals for balcony cabins.

I was very lucky for those opportunities to come along and also very lucky to be able to take advantage of them. Three experiences to be cherished.

9. LONDON AGAIN (1976 AND 2017)

The baggage carousel moved around, empty. The bags had been collected, but we were still waiting for one more item. The closed metal doorway beside the carousel held our attention.

It's different at every airport. Each time I get a foreboding feeling that things might not go as planned and start preparing myself for Plan B or even C. The feeling worsened at Heathrow as the minutes rolled by. We'd been travelling for twenty-three hours, a taxi was waiting, and I needed that mobility scooter to get me around. It was the first day of our four-week holiday and the scooter was an essential item. I wanted to get out of the airport wheelchair too. I'd been sitting in it for far too long.

I took a few photos of the empty space and steel doors to ease my anxiety and distract my mind. Finding my scooter had never taken this long before but, this was Heathrow International Air Terminal, one of the busiest airports in the world. Everything else had run so smoothly. It was surprising. I should be patient, I told myself. Just wait.

I'd been to London before, around 40 years prior, on a gap term. I was young, fresh, and new to overseas travel. I arrived in London from Montreal after spending a month travelling across Canada, but I cannot remember anything in particular about Heathrow Airport.

I arrived in Heathrow the day before Christmas Eve in 1976. It thrilled me to see green grass as we flew in. The Canada I'd just left had been a colourless grey turning white before the snow finally fell. Seeing green grass was wonderful, and I'd forgotten what a simple pleasure it was.

Someone from the Walkabout Club—a club I joined because I was travelling alone—met me at the airport and escorted me to an old hotel which felt safe and friendly with lots of other Australians staying there. It seemed like the place to stay for university students that came from all over the world. We each had a clean bed, and there was a bar with inexpensive pub food, a public telephone, and a mailbox. We were also in a great location near Hyde Park, close to an underground Tube stop—everything a student needed.

Years later, in the summer of 2017, I was travelling with Sue. We'd booked a taxi transfer and a hotel at St James Square, a place with a few more rating stars than my first old hotel. But we had to wait for my scooter to arrive before we could leave.

An airport baggage handler appeared, wheeling my scooter along by his side. Though not through the steel doors, as we'd been told. But thank goodness, my scooter had arrived. With big smiles, we thanked the man.

'Oh, good,' the mobility assistance woman added. She needed to go elsewhere with the wheelchair I was in.

Sue organised the scooter for me but after putting the battery in she sounded concerned. 'The light isn't coming on. It's not working. This tiller is wobbly too. Have you noticed it being this wobbly before?'

'No, I haven't. That's not right. Something's wrong,' I said, wiggling the tiller.

The mobility assistant quickly added, 'I'll get someone from the airline to help. Stay here, I'll be back.'

Sue and I couldn't understand what had happened, but my scooter was different from when I had last used it. We checked and rechecked the scooter, putting the battery in and out, turning the switch on and off. It didn't work. The tiller was wobbly too, but I couldn't ride it to see if it was a serious problem or not.

I needed to get my scooter working. After a week in London, we were off on a cruise to explore the UK. I needed it on the ship, going ashore, and on excursions. My mind raced with the alternatives I might have to consider.

Two airline staff from Qantas arrived and, after a quick explanation, they left, saying,

'We'll go to the airport's baggage desk and see what we can do. I haven't struck a problem with a scooter before. Are you sure the battery's not flat?'

'No, it can't be. It's been on board with me on the plane and it wasn't used much before we left in Melbourne. It doesn't make sense.'

The lost or damaged baggage counter was close to where we were waiting. The Qantas staff went over with the baggage tag for the scooter and then returned.

'He's going to phone a mobility aids repair place and see what he can organise.'

We waited and watched. The man behind the counter was on and off the phone and attending people in the queue. Things seemed to move slowly at Heathrow.

I wonder what it's like outside, I thought to myself. It had been a fine summer's day as we landed. I'd had enough of waiting inside, but it didn't look like we'd be getting outside soon.

The weather was cool in London back in 1976. It was winter at the time, and the only temperature I recorded in my diary was plus 5°C on the day I arrived. I was careful to put the plus sign in front of the 5°C after experiencing the negative temperatures I'd been travelling in for so long. In Saskatoon it had gone down to minus 34°C.

The first four days visiting London were unusual—on Christmas Day and Boxing Day I was in a daze from my first experience of jet lag. But I got out to explore because it was London and I wanted to see so much. I was excited to just be there.

I walked through Green Park and under the Wellington Arch to gaze in amazement at the buildings of Buckingham Palace, a place I'd seen so many times on TV. Westminster Cathedral is a must over Christmas, and I walked through Hyde Park where the trees were leafless, but the grass was green. During my time there, I could fit in so many famous sites and got a good feel for what London is all about.

Then I left on a bus tour of Europe for four weeks.

'The place they rang said they don't deal with Luggie scooters and they suggested we contact the supplier in Leeds.' The supplier was 350 km out of London. I don't recall ever visiting Leeds but, despite the allure of new places, I didn't feel like checking it out this time. The first week of this trip was just for London. We weren't interested in that idea.

'He's going to try some other places in between serving other people.'

Time was passing and someone from the waiting taxi had been sending messages.

'How long will you be?'

We had trouble keeping the car waiting. But we couldn't leave yet, as we had no means and no plan.

I responded with, 'Sorry, we don't know.'

We waited for more enquiries to be made.

When I arrived in London after the bus trip in 1977, I hadn't come from Heathrow but the port of Sheerness after a ferry trip from Vlissingen near Amsterdam. The new year had started in Bordeaux, and I'd been travelling around Europe with a hotel change almost every night. A bus left from the port to London's Victoria Station, where I made my way to the Walkabout Hotel again. I enjoyed staying in one place for a while.

That second time was different. The place wasn't completely foreign, and I wasn't on my own. I'd made friends on the bus tour around Europe and we explored places together. I didn't have to start from the beginning with every conversation I had.

Four of us banded together on the tour—three young teachers and me. We were the only single women on the trip. The rest were recently married or on their honeymoons, so their priorities were different. They also loved partying into the night. But our gang didn't want to go out partying. Our days were full of wonderful new scenes and experiences, so we didn't have much energy left at the end of the day. I wanted to stay awake as the bus travelled through Europe to see the countryside we were travelling through. I didn't want to sleep on the bus in the day and go out at night. The teachers felt the same.

In London, we visited the Tower of London, Madame Tussauds, and other sites I'd missed before. We went to the British Museum, where I loved seeing the mummies. I had never seen anything like them before. We went to see Agatha Christie's *The Mousetrap* murder mystery play in the West End. We also shopped at Harrods for a souvenir.

Everyone, except me, left after a week and I went to Heathrow Airport to see them off. In my diary, I noted it had been an odd day, full of sad goodbyes and learning about the IRA bombs going off in London. But I was undisturbed and left the next day with a Brit Rail Pass and a Youth Hostels handbook going around England, Scotland, and Wales on another adventure.

We were not on an adventure at Heathrow Airport in 2017!

We had to wait for a solution to my scooter problem but couldn't wait there any longer. After much discussion, we left the arrivals area with two Qantas staff members helping us to the taxi. One pushed me in the wheelchair through the airport, Sue wheeled our bag, and another person pulled my scooter along. They had rung our London hotel and organised a wheelchair to be waiting there. Sue, the defunct scooter and luggage, and I piled into the taxi and left the airport wheelchair behind with the staff.

We left with the suggestion to contact the Luggie scooter supplier on Monday and organise for mine to be collected and taken to Leeds for repair. But getting it back by Thursday before leaving for Dover to board the ship might not be possible. In the back of my mind, I had had enough and thought we'd ask the concierge at the hotel to help us. We'd just get to the hotel.

Besides, we were meeting up for dinner with our friends from Germany and the time was closing in. They'd flown over to join us for a few days. I figured the hotel wheelchair should get me to dinner.

The hotel staff were fantastic. I was met with a wheelchair as soon as the taxi pulled up and my scooter was taken to the concierge. We checked in and the concierge was going to ask the maintenance department for help. We left the scooter in their hands.

Not long after, Sue pushed me in the wheelchair to meet Thilli and Anni. It was great to see our friends again. We'd met them in 2011 on a cruise to the Arctic and Svalbard and had remained good friends ever since. We try to catch up with each other at least once a year somewhere in the world. They loved travelling too.

Sue pushed me from Piccadilly Circus to the restaurant. Thilli and Anni were used to something going wrong with the scooter, and we just chatted as usual after a brief explanation.

When we came back after dinner, the concierge said the mechanic wanted the charging unit for the battery. Sue went to the room and soon came back. We attached it to the scooter and plugged it into the power socket to show the concierge how it worked.

'Oh, my goodness, look, it switches on now! The light comes on. It's working. But the battery isn't flat. It's nearly full. Look at the indicator.' We disconnected the charger. The light still came on.

'It's fixed! How did that work?'

'Maybe the scooter parts were too cold after being in the hold for so long?' Sue suggested. We were on the same plane from Melbourne, so that was possible.

'Perhaps it just needed a kick start from real electricity,' I proposed. The concierge watched and nodded. All I could say was, 'Gee, that's great thanks.'

'Let's see how it goes.' I rode my scooter up to our room. I'd forgotten about the wobbly tiller.

I thought it might be wobblier the next day but thought, let's just see what happens. Maybe it isn't that bad. At least it's going. Let's re-discover London.

The hotel at St James Square was in the perfect location—close to galleries, museums, parks, the Palace, Academy of St Martin-in-the-Fields, restaurants, shops, everything we wanted to visit.

It is also only a short way to the River Thames, and that's where we headed first. I wanted to walk along the river.

The Prudential Ride London, an annual cycling event, had just started. Young and old were out there on the eight-mile route around Buckingham Palace, Trafalgar Square, St Paul's Cathedral, and Waterloo Bridge. The streets were closed all day for traffic and the footpaths were fenced off for the ride. Families were everywhere, with thousands of people on their bikes going past famous places at their own pace. As we made our way past Admiralty Arch, the entrance to the Mall leading to Buckingham Palace, we saw so many people on bicycles.

The Prudential Ride London through Admiralty Arch

The fencing made crossing the roads on my scooter difficult, but it was great getting out even if the scooter was a little wobbly. We moved along at a good pace, exploring along the way.

We were meeting Thilli and Anni for a lunchtime concert in Southwark Cathedral, followed by a walk together along the river.

We left the bicycling area and walked towards the river to cross the nearest bridge. The lift at the base of the first bridge we came across was out of order. Luckily, we asked a nearby policeman for help who gave us another accessible route.

Once at the nearby Tube station, we followed signs along narrow concrete corridors that eventually led out onto the Blackfriars Bridge over the River Thames.

I'd only seen images of The Shard before, and there it was to my left in the distance as we crossed the bridge. The tall skyscraper of glass and jagged edges stood out, and I understood what a grand landmark it was. Renzo Piano has created an architectural masterpiece. Once on the south bank of the river, we turned left and continued walking alongside the water in The Shard's direction.

It started to rain; we were running late, and the concert was about to start. I spotted a hotel, and we went there looking for a taxi. The London cab waiting was the perfect size and layout for my scooter and us. But due to the changed traffic routes from the bicycle event, it took longer than expected to arrive at Southwark Cathedral on the southern end of London Bridge.

Inside the cathedral, the concert had started, and we quickly and quietly found seats. We saw Thilli and Anni seated further up. The choir sounded extraordinarily beautiful. I'd never seen or visited the cathedral before. It is a stunning building, inside and out. Built in Gothic style, the arched ceiling above the choir seemed to give an extra heavenly element to their voices.

The concert inside Southwark Cathedral

Although I'd been to London before, and more times since 1977, everything we were doing in 2017 was new.

I'd also never been to Borough Market next door to the cathedral, and the four of us went there after the concert. It had been the site of terrorist attacks a few weeks earlier. We were not put off by the attack and, in fact, were keen to go there to show no fear.

The market was packed, and people bustled amongst stalls of fruit, vegetables, flowers, and food with restaurants, bars and eating places surrounding them. It was a wonderful food market, but difficult to navigate on my scooter through the crowd. It was easier once out and back onto the Thames walkway.

We headed back and found ourselves outside the Tate Modern Art Gallery near Shakespeare's rebuilt Globe Theatre. But then it was raining again, and we went back over the River Thames on the new Millennium suspension footbridge.

Morris dancers were everywhere. I saw them first dancing in small squares and then happily singing in beer gardens. A festival or competition must have been on. Several groups, each with their own coloured dress, were happily striding along with bell pads on their shins, shirts, armbands, and sashes, with floppy hats and carrying sticks. They joined us as we made our way over the bridge in the rain.

On the Millennium Bridge with my scooter and Morris dancers in the rain.

The first day out in London on my scooter was great, but at the end of the day, I had to face it. Something was definitely not right.

'Something is wrong with the steering. I feel like I'm sliding over the footpath'.

Back at the hotel, in the early evening, I had a good look under the scooter and at the tiller for the first time. Nothing appeared to be out of place.

I posted photos to my Instagram, explaining my problems with the scooter at the airport, and lots of people in the 'Instagram family' made helpful suggestions. I updated them on the scooter glide problem. They gave me contact phone numbers of people in London, but none were Luggie.

Then, I remembered the time in Finland with Thilli and Anni when the front wheel kept falling off on old, cobbled streets and the tiller was wobbly. An Allen key helped then. The next day the four of us were going by train to visit Robin—an old friend who lived just out of London, for a barbeque lunch. Although it would be Sunday, we hoped a hardware or bicycle shop would be open along the way so we could get an Allen key.

The next day, I had to concentrate as we walked and scooted from St James Square to Kings Cross Station. It took us an hour and nothing remarkable stood out until we saw the magnificent buildings of St Pancras Station. It is full of Victorian-era engineering marvels and distinctive Gothic revival features—thank heavens it wasn't demolished as being mooted in the 1960s. Restoration of its railway buildings was finished in 2007 and they finished the hotel in 2011. It is now the home of the Eurostar fast train to Europe under the English Channel, a swish five-star hotel, apartments and shops. What a landmark.

Across the road at Kings Cross Station, we met up with Thilli and Anni and I went straight to the information desk and asked for mobility assistance. A friendly train assistant led us to the train going north-east to the county of Hertfordshire and laid out a ramp for me.

At our stop, Robin was waiting. With the sun shining and the brightly coloured flowers out in her town, we walked to her house, excitedly chatting. We hadn't seen her for over a year.

I asked Robin where a local hardware store might be, and she immediately brought out several Allen keys of her own. I picked one and tried it in the space under the tiller, between the two front wheels.

The screw was loose and took a while to tighten. Anni had a go too, using all her strength to make sure it was tight. Yes, that felt better. The problem seemed to be fixed, and I wanted to get my own Allen key in case it loosened again. The one I bought in Finland was at home because I didn't think I'd need it again.

'Take this one with you. We used it to put all the furniture together here. I don't imagine I'll need it again soon. You can give it back to me when we meet up in the Shetlands after your cruise.'

'Great. Thank you.' I put it in my handbag.

I don't recall using any tool when I was on my first overseas trip. On my trips to London forty years ago, I was shopping for things other than tools and Allen keys.

When I returned from my four-week rail trip around Britain in 1977, I was in London for the third time. It felt like I was living there. Two friends I'd been at boarding school with were living and working in London. They'd been away and had returned from their holiday 'on the continent'. I spent time at their flat, cooking, eating, talking, laughing, and going out. They were nurses and worked in hospitals, private ones where movie stars and Arab princes were patients. They also participated in some private nursing gigs where the job included a small flat within the house. They took me to many places as well as a few tourists spots they hadn't had time for yet. The day trip to Windsor Castle, Eaton, and Hampton Court only cost £1. In 2017, I noted it cost £50.

My first visits to London were a long time ago, but they left me feeling excited. London was familiar. I knew I'd be back.

Over the next few days, we explored London and met up with other old friends. Now and then I'd check the scooter's front wheel and every time it was loose, I tightened it. It became ridiculous.

'Why don't I email Scooters Australia to ask if their technician can give us some advice?'

Sue quickly agreed.

In the hotel room, I asked Sue to take a photo of where the problem was on the scooter, with me pointing, to send in an email.

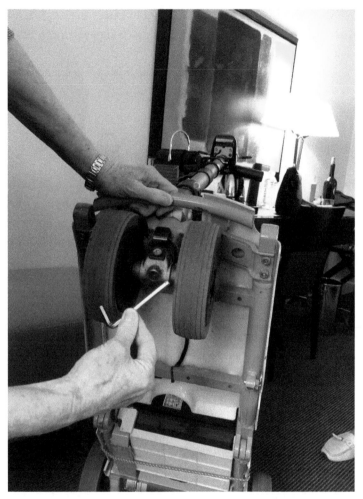

The Allen key and the problem section between the front wheels.

I heard back the next morning, with the recommendation to take the bolt out and put a couple of drops of a thread-locking compound (such as Lock Tite) into the space and put the bolt back in. I'd told them we were to board a ship, and they said the ship's engineering department should have some. But told me if I had time, I should buy some at a hardware store.

We were leaving London for the ship in Dover the next day, so I persisted in using my Allen key. The Lock Tite idea was new, and I wanted to wait until we got to the ship.

We left London for Dover the next day with a broken scooter. We stopped at Dover Castle on the way.

The bus tour to Europe in late December 1976 started leaving London for Dover.

In Dover, we boarded a hovercraft. I wrote in my diary: *incredible, flies over the water and takes twenty-six cars or more and only half an hour to get to France!* I felt the hovercraft rise up on the shore and move on to the water, leaving England and the white cliffs behind. I missed Dover Castle completely, heading for Boulogne.

I didn't know Dover Castle existed until this trip. It's probably the most significant and important castle in England, if not the UK. One would have thought I'd notice its imposing and obvious location on the top of the cliffs overlooking the port, the town, and the English Channel. On a clear day, they say, you can see the coast of France from the ramparts.

On this trip, I definitely wanted to see it, and it was an ideal opportunity. The ship didn't leave the port until the afternoon, and the trip from London would only take two hours. I booked a transfer to the Port of Dover that included a stop at Dover Castle for a few hours.

The driver of a small minivan dropped us at an area just off Castle Hill road that seemed to be a side entrance to the castle. The view from below the drawbridge up to the Castle was breathtaking and showed me how majestic it is.

So much of England's history is there. Many of the buildings within the castle walls have accessible paths between different sights. I was impressed.

We didn't have a lot of time, and the gale-force winds hurried us along. Taking the accessible path downwards, we arrived at the secret wartime tunnels and went inside one entrance to a hospital. We went on a tour of the hospital established during World War II. Seeing an operating theatre was fascinating. The wards were organised in tunnels dug into the soft chalk.

The gale-force winds continued and crossing the drawbridge almost swept me off my scooter. I had to stop three times while we were at the Castle to get out my Allen key and tighten the drifting front wheels.

We went down the steep hill back to the agreed pickup point where we were collected, loaded, and then deposited to the ship moored at the port to begin our cruise called Jewels of the National Trust.

Once aboard the ship, we went to Guest Services and explained the problem. Someone from the ship's maintenance department took the front wheel section off and disappeared with the bolt.

The young man wasn't away long before coming back with a cleaned bolt. He then worked on the scooter in front of me, cleaning the space and applying a thread binding liquid before screwing the bolt back in. I had to let it rest for at least a few hours or longer if possible.

We spent the first day of the cruise at sea, so my scooter wasn't needed ashore. I used my two walking sticks for short distances on board. We went to lectures, read in the library, and let the scooter's front wheels sit undisturbed. I didn't move it for 24 hours just to be sure.

The next day, we were in the Newhaven port for Edinburgh and the scooter was in perfect condition. I could ride to the adjacent port of Leith and visit the wheelchair accessible Royal Yacht Britannia, making a great start to the cruise.

The scooter did well for the next three weeks around England, Scotland, Wales and Ireland visiting some outstanding National Trust castles and gardens. The cruise finished back in Dover, where the historic castle now stood out for me. We then went to London, flying to the Shetlands and returning, before flying home. I forgot there was ever a scooter problem.

Returning to London again in 2017, I expected a different experience but not as different as it worked out. London has seen me at many ages, stages, and circumstances of life. Each time was unique, and it was unique again. After forty years I thought it might have changed for the worst, but it hadn't. Even for an older, more experienced traveller, with MS and a mobility scooter, it was just as wonderful.

10. A SHETLAND WALK (2017)

When I was invited to visit the Shetlands, I jumped at the chance. I'd never been, but whenever I'd heard anything about the place, I wanted to go.

Robin told us her grandfather came from a croft there, before he moved to Australia in the 1800s. 'I'd like to find where he lived,' she said.

'Yes, let's go.'

Exactly where in the Shetlands the croft was and how Robin might find it was an evolving adventure. She'd had a photo of a likely site in Deepdale, but the exact location was unknown.

The uncertainty didn't worry me. We were definitely going to the Shetlands to try to find the place. Sue and I had already booked a cruise for the following year around the UK. A trip to the Shetlands after the cruise fitted in really well.

Our adventure started when we arrived at Sumburgh airport on the main Shetland island, also called Mainland. The small Flybe propeller plane was a new experience, as was the extra-long boarding ramp on wheels for wheelchair users.

As we drove off in the hire car to meet Robin in Lerwick, we were suddenly on the runway. The hire car company warned us, but that didn't reduce our amazement when we drove across it. The airport tarmac was part of the highway. Looking left and right and up and down the runway, I immediately imagined a plane coming straight for us! But that didn't happen.

The thirty-minute drive from the far south of Mainland up the east coast to the middle of the island was through countryside I could never have imagined. Green land rolled down to the sea to join dark rocks and yellow sand, but it was also bare. It was beautiful and different to anywhere I'd been before. There was something unique about the place.

The main road was excellent. Locally called the oil road, built with money from recent drilling in the North Sea. The road snaked along the steep hilly sides of the coast as we headed north. What I saw from the passenger seat I loved immensely.

When we met with Robin, she told us about her investigations on her grandfather. Apparently, he had four wives and ten children in different countries! He was born and raised in a croft on the Shetlands before he left as a young man by boat for Canada. And then on to Australia and Fiji as the years (and wives!) rolled on.

But it was his time in the Shetlands we were concentrating on. Robin had an Ordnance Survey map to try to locate Deepdale and the croft. The croft no longer belonged to the family, but the abandoned ruins of the original stone house were supposed to be still there.

We sat down together at a big table in our apartment and poured over the map. There was a lot of open space with topographical lines indicating more than the usual ups and downs of hills and valleys. There were also symbols for bogs, dangerous cliffs, occasional dwellings, lakes, streams called burns (even a trickle of water was counted it seemed) and other unfamiliar (to me) parts of landscapes.

Robin was a keen walker and enjoyed long walks, some lasting a week. Sue was keen too, but I had stopped walking long distances and used my scooter instead–on level firm ground, not over bogs. My role in all of this was as a navigator and map reader, not as a walker.

'Have you brought a compass with you?' I asked, a bit concerned as to how we'd find the old croft in this wilderness.

'No, I didn't think I needed one.'

After looking at the map, I became a little worried. Robin pointed out a tiny dot that was Deepdale, but it was in the middle of nowhere with no roads or towns nearby, or other landmarks except bogs and burns. The main road near to it looked about twenty kilometres away. Robin had said earlier she'd been told the ground could be dangerous to walk on, and it was easy to fall over and get stuck in a bog. And walking alone was not a good idea. Robin had Sue, but she had her bad knee and was recovering from brain surgery.

To allay my anxiety all I could say was, 'I think we should buy a compass. They must sell a lot of them around here. There might be a map shop or a walking or outdoor shop somewhere in town. They should have compasses. We're going there first thing in the morning anyway to look around Lerwick, aren't we?'

'Yes,' Robin said. 'I'd like to show you a few interesting places I visited before you came, down on the waterfront where the old town is.'

'Is there a tourist information office?' Sue asked, wanting to find out more about the Shetlands.

'Yes, but I haven't been there yet. And look, at the end of the day it doesn't really matter if I get to Deepdale or not. I feel being here in the Shetlands is close enough to my grandfather. I didn't even think I'd get here, let alone to the croft. But I'd like to go to the tourist information office and talk about it.'

'We are definitely going to get you to that croft. We can drive as close as we can on the nearest road and I'll wait and mind things in the car while you two go on the walk, but I think you need to be prepared. To take water, a compass, a mobile phone, wet weather gear, some food, a whistle, and things like that. To be safe. Do they have a place to register for walks around here like they do in New Zealand and Tasmania?'

'No, I don't think so. Do you really think we'll need a compass? Let's just talk with people at the tourist information office first.'

Next morning, we began with a walk around Lerwick, starting at the small harbour and going out on the pier. I could see back to the old dark stone buildings of the town with a fortress on top of a small hill. My scooter found it easy going over cement paths and boardwalks.

Back in town, the old stone buildings were more interesting close up. Along with a few pubs there were shops selling local crafts, groceries and the usual things a small town has. The tourist information office was clearly signposted, and we all headed there. The old cobblestone paths and roads were manageable on my scooter and not too high on the bumpy-twisting scale.

At the tourist information centre there were handmade woollen items for sale including mobile phone covers, spectacle cases and the like. The woollen patterns were of local heritage designs and looked special. After admiring those I talked about the walk with one of the staff and then quickly realised it was really Robin and Sue who needed to talk with them.

'What did you say it was called again? Deepend? Or Deepdale of... or Deepdale via...?' the man asked.

'Oh, is there more than one Deepdale?'

'Yes...'

I left the conversation briefly to look at more of the craft works on sale and returned to see Robin with her map spread out. She had done her research. 'This is the Deepdale, where this little dot is. It's supposed to be a ninety-minute walk from the end of the road over bogs.'

'Okay.'

'Do you sell compasses here or know where we could buy one?' I interrupted.

The man in the tourist office was quick to inform us. 'You don't need a compass. There are no trees! You can see for miles around here and it's beside the sea. All you'll have to do is just look up and check which direction the sea is and head the opposite way inland. You'll see where you are going the whole way.'

'So, you think we'll be safe walking there?'

'Yes, of course.'

And 'of course' I thought too. No trees. That's what made this landscape different. No trees and you could see for miles.

Robin thought we should set out for Deepdale the next morning.

'I'll feel better when I've looked at exactly where it is. What it looks like before we tackle it,' she explained.

My job of navigating looked easy with Robin's detailed map. All the roads seemed well marked, most bitumen but some dirt and some just tracks. I was confident I could get us to the closest road.

With packed lunches made and backpacks organised, we set off in the morning. Before we left, I just double-checked if Robin had her mobile phone.

'Yes, I'll send a message on WhatsApp when we are out on the walk, if we decide to do it.'

We drove off onto the main road and headed south from Lerwick. After a little while I asked, 'Have you got water?'

'No, I forgot that,' said Sue. 'We'll have to buy some on the way.'

I pointed to a supermarket on the outskirts of Lerwick. 'Let's get some here.'

'There should be a shop later in a town nearby. We'll buy a few bottles then,' Robin chirped in.

After going south for a while, we turned right onto the road going west. At the highest point on top of the range, we stopped to have a better look at the view. We'd left the east coast behind us and were now facing the unique landscape of the west coast. Green farmlands still rolled down but with extremely tall steep cliffs on reaching the sea. Between the cliffs two protected bays with a peninsula in the middle, leading to an island, stood out–St Ninian's Isle, I noted on the map.

Along the way we stopped to take photos of the occasional farmhouse sitting on treeless green countryside with brightly coloured flowers in the garden. Any sized gully was signposted as a 'burn', while a few wooden boards over a trickle of water were marked as a 'bridge'.

The road became narrower and narrower. The few turn-ins we saw at the beginning to let other traffic pass, becoming none. With no other vehicles on the road, we arrived at a dead-end by the sea. There were three houses, a paddock, one beach, steep cliffs, a very steep grassy hill and a no-parking sign. 'Where is the town?'

'This is the town!' On the map there are only three dots. Three dots-three houses. No town. No shops.

Robin and Sue walked down to a large farm shed where two men were working outside to ask for information.

Sitting in the front passenger seat I watched them talking with an older and a younger man both dressed in singlet tops and overalls beside some farm machinery. It was a lovely sunny day. No need for arms to be covered on these men. I was rugged up in the car with a coat on.

Everyone chatted with more and more animation as time went on, pointing to the hill and laughing.

Robin came back and told me the father and son knew where Deepdale was. You just go up over that hill, up and down another hill, go past some water and up another smaller hill.

'I couldn't quite follow all the exact directions. But they didn't seem to think it would be a problem for us.' The father in particular knew so much about the place, and Robin was thrilled.

They also said to just park the car back at the dead end to one side of the road. Don't worry about the no-parking sign. Then Robin said she was going with the young man to their house to get some water for the walk. The inclination to always carry water on a walk must have been ingrained in us as Aussies with outback tales of heat and demise.

When we parked again, Robin excitedly told us that the men said on the last hill you'll see some stone ruins in the distance and to head for those. And to allow for a couple of hours.

'Okay, what's the time? Let's synchronise watches. It's 11:30am,' I said. 'The steep hill over there with a burn in the gully leads in the direction of Deepdale on the map too.' Pointing to the hill, I was keen to play my part. 'Here, take the map with you.'

'Alright we'll head off. If it takes ninety minutes each way. That's three hours and I think we need to allow more time to watch out for the uneven ground. I want to spend some time at the croft too, looking around, taking a few photos and thinking of my grandfather. That's at least four hours. I'll send you a WhatsApp when we get there.'

Using my walking sticks, I walked to the fence stile to see them off. At the stile there was a sign with a map for a heritage walk. It showed a track to the cliffs (marked 'Dangerous Cliffs Beware') that went to the left. Both Sue (and especially Sue) and Robin had a lot of trouble climbing over the stile. They were laughing so much at how much trouble they were having just getting started. Then Robin headed off to the left and Sue quickly said, 'No I think we go straight up here.' Oh, my goodness, I thought. I hope they get to the right place and back okay!

After we posed for some photos, they headed up the hill looking and waving back at me. I could still hear laughter as they climbed the hill and watched until they disappeared.

Sue and Robin at the top of the hill going to the croft

On the way back to the car I appreciated the small, almost hidden beach from a different angle, with steep rocky cliffs on either side. The three houses sat right on the beach. What a wonderful place to live.

Inside the car, my mobile phone had no bars of reception! All I could do was wait. It was about time for lunch, anyway.

After an hour or so, I went for a walk to a shed nearby. Sue told me about a horse she'd seen inside with a foal. The farmer told her they were on a special diet as they'd eaten too much, and we were not to feed them. I found two overweight Shetland ponies, mother and daughter. At least Sue had seen a Shetland pony, I thought. She'd been trying to find one ever since we landed on the island.

Back at the car I was reading a book when a WhatsApp message from Robin came in. My phone still registered no mobile phone bars, but there was a message.

We are at the croft, having a quick lunch then heading back. All good. An hour to get back, probably. I noted it was at about 2pm on Monday 21 August 2017 for the finding of the croft. I was thrilled for them.

I replied and continued reading my book.

At about 3:15pm I kept an eye out. Exactly four hours after they left, they reappeared at the top of the hill. I took photos as they came down the hill with their jackets off tied around their waists, wearing only short sleeves (I still had a warm jacket on). They moved slowly and carefully over the uneven ground. One of Sue's lower legs was covered in mud above her runners. They both looked a little tired but elated.

'The old stones of the croft buildings were still there. You could see where the original house was. It was much bigger than I thought and had a wonderful view down the valley to the sea. Look at the photos I took.' Robin was so pleased.

I looked and wow, yes, that croft would have had a fantastic view down a small green grass valley with small waterways rolling down to the sea. It was in a stunning location.

The views in Robin's other photos taken along the way, especially looking back to the sea, told me how silly I was. They could never have got lost. The way was easy to see. They didn't need a compass. It was just over a few hills.

Robin also wanted to try to visit a cemetery she'd read about on our way back to Lerwick.

'It's supposed to be somewhere here.' Robin pointed to an area on the map called Bigton, not far away, where there were a few scattered dots.

After spending some time in the Bigton area without success, we eventually turned onto a dirt track and went down to the bay when we suddenly spotted a marking on the map, 'ctry'. Close to the water's edge, the road suddenly turned right and headed out to a bluff by the sea. Set back from the cliffs, low stonewalls were arranged in a rectangle with a large flat area of gravel beside it.

Inside the grounds was a well-kept cemetery with about fifty weathered gravestones, all with difficult-to-read inscriptions. Dried lichen covered the hand-hewn upright stones, embedding all the hollows of the writing. The small cemetery could not have been the island's main cemetery. It seemed to be a local one and old. Some of the names I made out were those on businesses I'd seen in town. Robin wandered around on her own, taking her thoughts with her. Over the wall, from inside the grounds were long views out to sea past headlands jutting out. The Shetland people had many close connections with the sea, and these graves were still close.

On the way back we stopped at the nearby tidal island of St Ninian's Isle. Robin and Sue walked from the mainland across the sandy peninsula with water breaking gently on both sides to get to the island. I sat looking at the blue ocean and bay scenery, the green island and the sand, watching Sue and Robin. When I got up to stretch, I noticed the bench seat I was sitting on had a memorial plate on the back. The plate read–*KESTER WIGRAM, 1959–2010. A free spirit.* I read later he was an adventurous New Zealand kayaker who went missing after parking his car at Bigton and entering the water at St Ninian's Isle beach. His body was never found, but there was talk of a skull being found some time later. His ex-wife was reported as saying if he could choose a place to die, it would have been the sea. Such was his love for it.

My scooter sat in the boot for that day. But it was still essential for other outings.

It surprised me I could ride my scooter around the Neolithic Jarlshof site with its prehistoric buildings dating back to 2,500 BC. I was even more surprised to get inside some of the remnant rock living quarters on my scooter.

At Sumburgh Head, where a historic lighthouse sits up high, ten percent of all Britain's seabirds breed in the cliffs there. From the visitor car park at the base, there is a very long steep haul to the top which I didn't think my scooter would make. So, I was thrilled to discover there are two disabled parking spots at the top. Next to that car park the viewing deck was scooter accessible and had superb views of bird breeding sites and birds happily flying about.

We drove to Scalloway on the west coast to visit the museum next to a castle, but it was closed, and the small area of castle ruins was fenced off. But we saw a pair of Shetland ponies being fed by their owner in the paddock beside them. We made a beeline for the woman (and the ponies to pat!) and chatted with her as she fed her beloved ponies. One was pregnant, she explained, not overweight. Heck, it was difficult to understand her accent. It was even more difficult than it is to understand people on the TV series *Shetland* with such broad Scottish accents.

However, speaking with the locals was a treat. Some accents were stronger than others, all different to me. Despite my full concentration, I could only understand a little of what they were saying. Those who had been living there longer seemed to have the strongest and most unique of all Scottish accents I'd ever heard.

Down on the small Scalloway harbour front there was a monument to the Shetland Bus, the name given to the fishing vessels making repeated trips to evacuate Norwegians from Bergen during the Nazi invasion. It was dangerous as the war played out around the seas of Shetland with its lighthouse playing a pivotal role. It made me realise so much had happened on the Shetlands. Robin's grandfather was in there somewhere, too.

The weather while we were there was fabulous - shining, blue skies and warm. When it was time to leave, it started to change but the weather was to be the least of our worries.

On the last day when we were about to drive into Sumburgh airport, there was a message on Robin's phone. 'Dear me, the cleaner in the apartment has found a plastic bag with shoes in it. Could they please have an address to post them?'

We were flying to London via Edinburgh that morning and arriving at Heathrow at about 4:30pm. It was Sue's birthday. I booked an airport hotel for the night and a restaurant for a surprise dinner, before our flight home to Melbourne the next morning. My infusion at the day centre was the day after. This was the only flight leaving the Shetlands linking up with the flight home.

'What'll we do?' Sue asked.

'It doesn't matter,' I said, thinking I'd have to wear a pair of runners or sandals to dinner instead. 'It's more important we get home tomorrow.'

'I think I'll go back and get them,' said Sue, looking at her watch. 'Can you go in and find out what time they close check-in?'

'That will take ages, we haven't got time.'

There was umming and ahhing. 'If I go faster than I've been going, I should be back in time,' Sue said. Robin suggested she go with Sue because they'd be quicker if she ran in to get the shoes.

'Go in and find out what the last check-in time is and text Robin when you find out. I can always turn around if it looks impossible.'

I was left with the scooter on the airport terminal footpath as Sue and Robin drove off. This will be a good test for me, I thought. Sue usually puts the scooter up and gets it ready for me to ride. I had a bit of practice of doing it on my own when Sue was in hospital for a week, and it wasn't too difficult. I soon rode inside the terminal.

There was no one in the queue to check-in and a friendly-looking woman beckoned me forward. I quickly explained what was happening.

'Plenty of time to get to Lerwick and back. When I have to work, I can do it in 20 minutes. They'll be alright. Last check in is 11:15am for the 11:45am. Where would you like me to bring the wheelchair for you to get into? What about over there at the table in the café?'

'Wow, that is so nice of you thank you, yes.' I finished checking in, had my boarding pass, and rode the scooter over to the café. As soon as I was there, I sent an SMS to Robin to tell her the times.

Sometime later I received a message back *Passed Tesco, on way back*. That was the supermarket just out of Lerwick where we didn't buy the bottles of water. Still a long way away.

I had to send another message. 'See you on the plane. Man coming to take me through early. See you there.' I hoped!

I went through security soon after and sat in a wheelchair at the departure gate looking out at the windy, overcast, terrible weather rolling in and worrying Sue and Robin wouldn't get back in time. I just sat and waited. What could I do? Just wait. The 11:15am check-in deadline passed.

I was drifting off into another world, just sitting and waiting, trying to remain calm.

'Hello!' Sue said standing beside me. 'You'll never believe what security we had to go through. They were so thorough. I had to get out all your medications from the carry-on bag and put them in a special clear plastic bag... then they found something else to ask about... I had to answer so many questions… everything was everywhere… you should have seen it!'

'We were caught behind a big truck going into Lerwick would you believe. Of all the times!' Robin exclaimed.

'We almost didn't make it,' Sue added honestly. 'As soon as we'd checked in and received our boarding passes, the woman at the desk said the flight was now closed, no more allowed. How close was that?'

Not long after we arrived at Heathrow, we were soon enjoying Sue's surprise dinner. I didn't have to wear old sandals or runners as my shoes had made it with me.

We had a great time on Mainland in the Shetlands. We all loved the place and would like to go back. Robin did mention her grandfather moved to nearby Fair Isle for a while!?!

11. IN HAWAII WITH MUM (1996 – 2018)

We were going to Hawaii with Mum again. Except this time, she was in a small, sealed box. Well, at least one-third of her was. Her dying wish was for her ashes to be divided and spread in three places. Honolulu was one of them.

According to US customs requirements, we could bring her ashes on the flight as hand luggage. We just had to have her death certificate and make sure the crematorium labelled the ashes in a non-metallic container able to pass through TSA x-ray machines. Hawaiian Airlines was in fact very encouraging of the idea on their website *'we welcome...'*

My mother loved Hawaii. She'd been more than once and dreamed of living there for six months of the year. She had a huge attraction to the place, especially for the hula championships and hula dancing.

'Look at those hips moving,' she'd say with a wide, bright cheeky smile. We first learned how important the hula was to Mum when we saw the videos from her first trip in 1978. She loved watching people hula dance, especially small children, and she loved us watching with her.

Mum's videos showed enormous crowds on the opening day of the hula championships along the footpaths of Kalakaua Avenue, the main street in Waikiki. People leaned out from the road's edges to get a view of the procession. The large floats had people of all ages, sizes and sexes hula dancing and playing ukuleles. Girls and men dressed as warriors paraded between the floats. Frangipani flowers were everywhere.

Because Mum enjoyed being in Hawaii so much, she made sure the whole family went back with her at least once. That happened in 1996.

The hula championships were not on, so Mum took us to see some hula at the Polynesian Cultural Centre on the north of the island of Oahu.

We sat in open-air stands rising up from the stage, watching and listening in the scorching sun. Mum made her own announcement following the ones over the loudspeaker, 'Here they come'. Every group made its own entrance-the Hawaiian Islands, Samoa, Tonga, the Cook Islands, Tuvalu, New Zealand, Easter Island, Tahiti, the Marquesas and other islands.

They came out with flowers everywhere-around their necks, in their hair, on their arms and grass skirts and on poles held high as banners. One group followed another singing, playing music and dancing. Tanned and part naked, some wore half coconut shells on their breasts. Some had generous waists, while muscles were more prominent in others. Shell necklaces and bracelets added to the decoration.

But the cultural centre wasn't enough hula for Mum, so she took us to Kapi'olani Park in Honolulu. The large Waikiki Shell amphitheatre had been built there for the Kodak Hula Show and other hula events. The Kodak show started in 1937 when someone thought Hawaii's hula dancers would make great photo opportunities for visitors. Millions of people came from all around the world to see the show and have their photos taken in front of the shell. There must have been a lot of Kodak film and photos sold!

When we were there, the crowds watching the hula demonstrations weren't as large as in Mum's videos. It was probably early signs of some waning popularity.

Mum also loved walking around Waikiki in the warmth and checking out quirky things for sale along Waikiki Beach strip and in the market. She couldn't resist buying items for herself or for gifts. She just loved 'tricky' things.

The International Market Place sold a huge variety of products – jewellery, clothes, food, knick-knacks and all things Hawaiian at bargain prices. Some paths were dirt with trees growing and everything was haphazard, but the result made the place seem like a crazy world of its own. Entertainers popped up singing and all sorts of events took place there.

One of many things Mum bought was a large, coloured handbag shaped like a fish. It was bright yellow and blue with a long handle going over her shoulder. Mum would flash the fish as she walked along the street and enjoyed getting on buses and going for rides, proudly showing it off. She carried an assortment of funny things in the fish handbag that would come out at an appropriate, or inappropriate time, depending on how one saw the situation! These included bright red plastic lips she'd wear on her mouth and a set of plastic false teeth that made a clacking sound when the attached tong-like handle was moved up and down. I think it was meant to be some kind of salad server.

If we looked over at her when we were on the bus, she'd move her shoulder and make the fish handbag move up and down while raising her eyebrows at the same time! I didn't know quite what to think.

Working as a real estate agent back home, Mum had a Hawaiian-style wooden nameplate on her desk with many quirky things sitting beside it. Items were also placed waiting in the top drawer, ready to be pulled out if needed for a story, making a point, getting a laugh or for some other inspirational opportunity. Mum loved working in real estate. She was a recent graduate, attending TAFE in her fifties, and the freshness and enthusiasm was always there.

Another thing Mum loved doing was saying the name of the first king of the Hawaiian Islands, King Kamehameha. She pronounced it as King Kamaya-maya-maya-maya... we all followed suit, saying the same and often. King Kamaya-maya-maya-maya-maya...

Then there was 'the Duke'. Duke Kahanamoku-now a nine-foot bronze sculpture at an entry point on to Waikiki Beach. He was the Hawaiian Olympic swimming champion and father of international surfing. Everyone visiting Honolulu goes past the statue at some stage, sometimes several times a day.

Both my brothers and I were swimmers and surfers and knew of the Duke. We thought Duke Kahanamoku was wonderful, nicknaming him either 'The Duke' or 'The Big Kahuna'.

But it was the hula dancing and hula shows Mum loved most. She bought a clock with a hula girl at the base that sat in her lounge room doing the hula non-stop.

With any mention of the word Hawaii, Mum's eyes would light up. The tricky things she kept in her fish bag would come out at Christmas time, birthdays or any family event.

We understood why mum wanted to leave some of herself there, a part to live in Hawaii all year round. My two brothers and I took a few years after she died to organise a date for us all to be there.

Sue and I stayed at the iconic 'Pink Palace' or Royal Hawaiian hotel in Honolulu. It is right on Waikiki Beach, built back in 1927 and Mum and I stayed there, over twenty years before. It seemed fitting. The views of the ocean and beach from our room were superb.

On our first night, a few days before the get-together, Sue and I headed to the Mai Tai Bar at the Royal Hawaiian for a sunset drink, sitting at a table under hot pink umbrellas overlooking the beach. We had been there before with Mum having cocktails.

Before too long it was dark, subtle lighting came from the lantern flames, the waves were breaking gently on the shore and I turned to see Sue fast asleep at the table! I think the mixture of several island rums in her Mai Tai, hit her more quickly than the bourbon, rum, curacao and fruit juice in my Okolemaluna Itch! It had been a long day with an overnight flight arriving early that morning, so we staggered off to find my scooter, then made it back to our room for an early night.

The next day I couldn't help but notice a lot of different Asian families in matching Hawaiian clothes walking around the hotel. People of all ages and both sexes-small children up to grandparents-were dressed in identical Hawaiian flower-patterned shirts, pants or dresses in exactly the same colour for one party and another colour for another group. Some were even walking out on the streets. I thought it might be for weddings or some special family event. It was different.

Outside the Royal Hawaiian, I found an elevated pathway running along the beachfront for my scooter to explore. It was accessible except for one set of steps along the way. The tide must have been high as the ocean waves splashed up and over the walkway. The stop, near the steps on my scooter was a photo opportunity with the view behind back to Diamond Head.

Me on my scooter in Hawaii

I'd never seen Waikiki Beach with so much water over it. Earlier in the year I'd heard the news of cyclones in the area causing flooding, but even more recent news explained it was an ongoing problem for the beach with sea levels rising due to climate change.

The walkway only extended as far as the adjacent sister hotel, with its shopping mall and pools area. But both hotels were on large pieces of beachfront land with gardens and lawns, so the walk went a fair way. At the infinity pool, everyone was on the same yellow beanbags positioned or getting ready to position themselves at the edge looking out at the ocean and sky. The three blue colours were striking with the yellow and the horizon line dividing them.

The infinity pool with yellow beanbags

We left the pool and beach and headed out across the road for the International Market Place. I was shocked. It was gone. The stalls and entertainment areas, there since 1956, had been removed, bulldozed I imagined. Now in its place were high-end luxury shops in a shopping mall several stories high. The quirkiness and old Hawaiian vibe was missing, and I thought it was sad. I read later the market closed in 2013 for complete renovation and reopened in 2016. Things had changed.

There were no hula shows in the park either. The last performance in the large Waikiki Shell was in 2002. After sixty-five years, the Kodak Hula Show was no more. The reasons given for stopping the show were 'dwindling visitor numbers because of fears after the 9/11 attacks on mainland USA and changing economic conditions.' But times and tastes had changed too, I could see.

'Hula is the language of the heart and the heartbeat of the Hawaiian people,' one Hawaiian King was supposed to have said. But in Honolulu the hula seemed to beat mostly for tourists in hotel resorts. I was thrilled to learn the Hawaiian people are still telling their story and hold serious hula competitions on the other islands of Maui and Hawaii.

In Honolulu, on Oahu, all the family was there for mum's farewell. She came on the plane from Brisbane with one brother, tucked away in a small container. The family of ten with mum in 1996 had grown to seventeen with ages between a few months and seventy.

I rode my mobility scooter to the gathering near 'the Duke'. We sat at the nearby wooden tables and the setting sun over the ocean was a perfect scene to share a drink, talk of mum and bring out some of her tricky things. One brother wore the fish handbag and new matching thongs bought for the occasion.

One brother with the fish handbag and new thongs

It was simple and relaxed, no real ceremony, a get-together where we spoke about Mum, what she loved and the funny things she'd said.

We placed a few of her ashes in the water at Waikiki Beach so we could imagine her floating out to sea looking back at the Pink Palace, the Duke and the beach strip. She could float off and travel around the other islands too and see the hula competitions. We left a small part of her there. Mum would have loved it all.

12. SCOOTER IN THE SNOW (2018)

When we landed at Churchill Airport in Canada, it was snowing. In late October 2018, freezing temperatures had arrived in the south-western corner of Hudson Bay.

From the plane window I could see my unloaded scooter on the ground outside.

'Quick!' I called out to Sue, who was removing our things from the overhead locker. 'I can see them from here. They're trying to put the scooter up in the snow! I can see them pulling at the tie and trying to lift the seat. You have to stop them. They'll break it.'

Sue rushed to the exit door and went down the steps to tell the two men to stop.

'It won't work in the snow, you'll have to take in with the luggage,' she said.

I slowly followed and met Sue at the bottom. Holding her arm with one hand and my walking stick in the other, we moved carefully over ice and snow to get inside the terminal.

Enormous signs were up on the wall 'Welcome to Churchill, the Polar Bear Capital of the World'. Yes, we were there to see the polar bears-in their natural habitat this time. Our small group tour began with a night in Winnipeg, followed by a charter flight to Churchill the next morning.

I felt we'd missed out seeing polar bears on the Svalbard trip in 2011. There were only two or three and they were so far away and in such poor health after being stranded on the warmer western side of the island, it sort of didn't count.

Sixteen of us were gathering at the airport to wait for our next instruction. I wondered where my scooter was after the attempt to put it up in the snow. Maybe it'd been taken directly to the hotel with our luggage? Maybe it was on the bus ready for our first excursion? It was in Churchill somewhere. It wasn't a big place to get lost in with a population of less than nine hundred.

Inside the terminal were many vacant seats, and the building wasn't like the usual airport terminal. Not just because of the empty seats but also because it was one open space, like a huge departure gate waiting area. Something was missing. It wasn't until we were there, days later, when I realised there were no screening machines, no metal detectors, no security personnel and no baggage areas. What happened at this airport seemed to be very different. I found out more on the way back.

Our tour guide directed us to a small bus just outside. I used my walking sticks to walk the short distance to the exit. The pathway outside was covered in snow over ice, and I needed Sue's arm to lean on. Inside the bus, I saw my scooter placed ninety degrees upright against the front seat. Phew, I felt better after seeing it, even though it was in an odd position. Its wheels still had snow on them.

Churchill's township is small, but its surrounds are enormous. It sits in a remote location where the Churchill River, fed from fresh water in the south, enters Hudson Bay. We'd flown over that waterway and land for hundreds of kilometres. It was a treeless flat landscape of a myriad of tiny and medium-sized lakes in northern Manitoba. Hudson Bay collects thirty percent of all the water runoff in Canada.

The tour around Churchill was impressive. The local guide reminded us fresh water freezes faster than saltwater. The Churchill River and the Nelson River (further east) were the two main sources of fresh water that froze early and emptied their ice into salty Hudson Bay. The massive bay connects to both the Arctic and the North Atlantic oceans. Polar bears gather on Hudson Bay's shores, waiting for it to freeze so they can move over it to catch seals. Every year the bears move in a north-westerly direction to get to Churchill where the ice forms first, creating the largest known polar bear gathering in the world.

Churchill has an interesting history. Initially set up on the mouth of the river as a trading post by the Hudson's Bay Company, it is named after Lord John Churchill, a company member and one of the explorers who tried to find the Northwest Passage. It was once a large port and rail centre shipping grains grown on the prairies further south.

Its strategic position was important too. In 1942, Canada and the United States set up a military base there that served as a monitoring station in World War II. The airport, roads and other infrastructure were built to support it.

On the tour around Churchill, we stopped at a polar bear holding facility (a temporary polar bear 'prison' for bears that wandered into town, pending their release elsewhere), sites of old settlements alongside the bay and river, landmarks and other points of interest. I couldn't use my scooter as there was deep snow everywhere, so I used my walking sticks at every stop except for once, when it would have been too dangerous with the powerful icy winds blowing, and I remained in the bus.

Over the next five days, my scooter stayed in the hotel room and never ventured out again. Before leaving Australia, I knew there might be snow in town by late October, but not necessarily. If it had snowed, I thought there might have been cleared footpaths. But snow was everywhere and there were no footpaths to clear.

Each day we went out on a Tundra Buggy. I read we'd be boarding it at a 'launching station' twenty minutes out of town. Not a launching pad, but there was one of those there too. The Churchill Rocket Research Range was on the way to our loading station. It was set up in 1954 for scientific research into the upper atmosphere, with a commercial spaceport being a real idea. Now it is a research facility and a National Historic Site of Canada, no longer used for rocket launches.

The Tundra Buggies were bus-like vehicles with enormous tyres holding their bodies high off the ground with big windows at the front and on the sides. The back had an outdoor wooden deck with a high balcony around it. This back section flipped down at the rear and was being reversed into the elevated station platform.

'Go to number six boarding area please and wait. There'll be plenty of room inside. The buggy seats forty, but with less than twenty you'll all get a window seat,' the tour leader explained as we got off the bus. There were a few pushy people in our group, so that was good to know.

I went down the bus steps and onto the snow to stand right in front of another set of wide steps leading up to the platform. With handrails it was easier to climb up than it looked, and all I needed was one walking stick. Once up on the flat wooden deck it was no trouble getting into the buggy. I'd been worried about how I'd get inside after seeing photos of the high vehicles.

As we were boarding the buggy, I looked out from the top of the deck and noticed the size of the enormous wheels on each of the buggies. They held the buggy up high and safe from any standing polar bears. We later learned adult male polar bears can measure up to ten feet.

It was below freezing outside, but lovely and warm inside the buggy. I thought I had enough warm clothing on to be outside, but not to the standard of that Canadian cold. Thank goodness the buggy was heated. There was plenty of room inside and with a toilet at the back, it was almost like a cosy mobile home.

After a safety briefing, we went out on the old military-built roads maintained to protect the natural tundra environment. An extensive area along Hudson Bay is protected, and we were going to enter the Churchill Wildlife Management Area. It is one of the largest protected wildlife management areas in Canada, home to annual polar bear gatherings and the most accessible place on earth to view polar bears in their natural habitat.

The adjacent land further east, Wapusk National Park, was established to specifically protect polar bear breeding grounds. It is now home to the largest land polar bear denning area in the world. The word 'wapusk' is Cree for 'white bear'.

Despite being called trails or roads, they were very rough with deep boggy pits now and then. The driver explained the Tundra Buggies at Churchill had been specially made for the purpose.

White on white, fur on snow, still or moving, a polar bear could be difficult to spot. Their long noses with black tips helped, as they raised their heads and noses even higher in stages to smell what was happening. Their sense of smell is extraordinary.

Their huge paws flicked forwards up and down at the ankle like ballet dancers with big round soft pads, but the bears had long claws at the end. They moved, gentle and quiet. We watched them turning over blocks of ice and searching underneath for tiny specks of food. They used their claws with care and precision.

At first, I photographed every polar bear I saw from whatever distance and whatever angle. Then we sat and just watched. The gigantic creatures didn't seem to mind. They'd walk around, sometimes curiously putting their front paws up on the tyres or rear bumper to look inside. They normally don't eat humans unless they're desperate. Apparently, we don't smell nice to them.

It was a privilege to sit there and watch them. At one stage I looked down into the eyes of a bear so near that I knew from the way he looked at me he was watching closely too!

In Churchill, our hotel and all the eating places were at least one hundred metres away from each other. I thought I'd use my scooter to go to and fro and wander around town, but with snow and ice and no scooter it turned out to be a very slow walking job.

Another surprise was the darkness at night. With only a few streetlights and slippery, thick ice, it was dangerous. Falling over would be very easy. We had to be careful. Careful not only to not slip and fall, but also to avoid any bears that might be roaming around town at night! Bears were spotted every night while we were there. They are very curious animals and will always check new things out. Luckily there is a local patrol that 'encourages' bears to get out of town. Failing that, they are caught and held in the facility before being flown back to 'their' area.

The first two nights when we walked the streets, we followed safety instructions to walk in groups, talk loudly to discourage attacks, stay in open areas and never walk alone, or take short cuts between houses or go into lanes. It was difficult walking with one walking stick and an arm to hold. But two walking sticks weren't stable enough. I was also freezing, especially my feet. Every slow step I had to measure and think through.

Several people in the group had severe walking difficulties. One stayed in the hotel room and had meals brought to her by friends. The guide said usually there was a bus available to take people at night, but for some reason he wasn't allocated one this time. Another tour group's leader told us it was too dangerous to walk and to get in the bus with her group. From the third night on, our leader had managed to score a small bus. It was so much easier, warmer and safer to be taken door to door.

In Churchill there was a small one-room museum and a National Parks information centre where we were taken briefly. If there was more time, we would have gone back to learn more, but it was too difficult to walk there. The best thing I saw at the information centre was a recreated polar bear den. It was made of sticks, other pieces of dead trees, mossy material and leaves. With a hole at the front, it was raised and set back into a boggy mound under snow and ice. Apparently, mother polar bears use the same den each season. Seeing the lifelike set up in the museum was a new sight for me. We weren't allowed to go anywhere near the real dens that are super protected.

Dog sledding was listed on our itinerary, but I thought I wouldn't be able to go. So, I went to watch. Or so I thought.

'I can't stand up', I told the operator.

'Well, just sit down in the front! No problem!' he quickly responded.

With a blanket over my legs sitting in front of a team of Alaskan huskies, it was a breeze. Yes, breezy too because it was colder on my face and neck with the dogs racing along. But pulling up my neck warmer and tightening my hat worked well. The excitement also helped take my mind off feeling cold.

At one stage a photographer leaned out from behind a tree and captured the moment.

Dog sledding in Churchill

The people in our tour group were a mix of British, American, Swedish and German with us as the only two Australians. Our accommodation was spread out in a number of different small hotels, but we came together for meals where we chatted more freely.

Then I really noticed Karen later in a gift store. She held three large soft polar bear toys and other mementos in her arms. She looked so funny, like a big kid at age forty. I laughed so much seeing her holding the bears, and everyone laughed when she said she wanted another one.

At the end of the trip, sitting at the airport waiting to board our plane, we started talking again. At the end of our conversation, I didn't know what to say. Karen started by telling me that polar bears held a special place in her heart ever since she was a child. She dreamed of seeing real ones. This was the last opportunity for her because she was dying. The trip with her family and close friends was a present for her birthday and to show how much they thought of her. She was so positive, matter of fact, and practical.

'What can I do?' she said. 'There's no more possible treatments.'

When we returned to Winnipeg, a bus came and quickly parked right alongside the steps from the plane. We just went down the steps, out of the plane, and up into the bus. It went straight back to the hotel. There was no airport terminal building to go through, no baggage carousel to collect luggage from, and no oversize luggage area to get my scooter out of. With the charter flights there was no need for passports, checks on the battery or baggage, or security. No one checked or asked questions about my lithium battery before boarding, and we carried it back to the hotel lobby where the scooter was delivered. Everything and everyone arrived at the hotel safely and quickly. Apparently, that's just what happens on charter flights. I like that!

With a mix of more than a few new privileged encounters on our trip, we rested at the hotel that night with much to be thankful for and reflect on.

13. SOUTHERN AFRICA CONFRONTATIONS (2018 – 2019)

Six of them stood there with their long necks straight and upright, heads facing and eyes looking, directly at us. They stepped forward, then waited, then advanced and then waited again until others caught up, all not moving their heads. This was a stare down, our guide informed us. The giraffes were not staring us down, rather the lions beside us who seemed to occasionally eyeball them back. So cool, pretending not to notice in this serious game. But the lions knew, watching them long before they came into our line of sight.

We were on a safari drive at Shamwari, ninety minutes by road from Port Elizabeth, South Africa, where our plane landed. We chose that private game reserve because of its rehabilitation and conservation work, revealed in the television documentary series *Wild & Woolly: An Elephant and His Sheep*. The story is about the extraordinary friendship between an orphaned baby elephant (Themba) and a sheep (Albert). The Shamwari Rehabilitation Centre rescued Themba and spent two years helping him return to the wild with the help of Albert. The series shows how the unlikely friendship grew to devotion and love in a more than heart-warming way.

The game drives at Shamwari start early before dawn or late in the afternoon around sunset, not in the middle of the day when it is hot and the animals rest. We were told to wear neutral coloured clothing, covering our arms and legs and not to stand up in the jeep, shout or talk loudly.

Our safari guide explained the animals' behaviour in a way that I had never heard before, and I understood the wild animal world in a whole new way. I loved learning about it.

The lioness calls the shots when hunting. She decides when and how to go for the kill. We sat in our open jeep near the pride of lions being eye-balled and watched for over an hour. The lions lay stretched out, yawning, nodding off occasionally, looking like they couldn't care less. The male seemed to only move to have sex with the lioness and the guide said that could be one hundred times a day. We certainly witnessed many times as we sat there! Then the lead female moved off to one side and ever so slightly toward the giraffes. The giraffes needed water from the watering hole nearby, and both groups knew that. The lioness disappeared silently to our right. The males moved later, one at a time, slowly and nonchalantly in the lioness's direction. The giraffes continued to move forward little by little with their eyes fixed on the lions.

All four of us in the jeep with the guide were fascinated. We were relaxed because we'd been told lions don't like humans to eat because the wild animals taste better and there were plenty of them about. But the guide also had a rifle within reach. He explained the giraffes might stop being attacked by staring down the lions.

The scene we were watching could go on for hours. If the lions weren't hungry, they might not bother too much if things became difficult. As much as we wanted to, we couldn't stay sitting there and left before it all ended to find some other wild animals to watch.

The open jeeps or special safari vehicles were high off the ground. I was concerned about how I would get in on my own, but I need not have worried. There was a safari vehicle loading dock with a ramp at reception. I could ride my scooter from our tented sleeping quarters along a concrete path to reception and go up the ramp onto a wooden deck. With the scooter parked in front of the reception hut, I could use my walking sticks from there. The safari vehicles pulled up to one side of the deck and it was simply a matter of just walking in and sitting down.

A large elephant with enormous tusks almost walked into the jeep with us one day too! We turned a corner on a narrow dirt road, in the middle of thick prickly acacia bush, to find an elephant in the middle of the road. He was close and towered over us.

The elephant we met on the road

We stopped immediately. I could have put my hand out to touch him as he came nearer but that thought never occurred to me. With our guide in charge we just waited patiently and watched.

The elephant kept on eating leaves, and branches with long, pointed thorns sticking out of them. Elephants loved eating these prickly bushes by wrapping their trunks around them, pulling branches off, or sometimes by pulling the whole bush out and holding that in their mouths while they chewed and swallowed.

A baby elephant nearby was trying to learn how to use its trunk, but it was so soft it just flopped around. He was soon more interested in chasing and playing with another youngster. The elephant walked past us, so close, and he didn't touch us either. The surrounding herd moved along too, decimating every bush in their wake and eating them. We waited, then followed a small group of elephants down the road to our next destination. Mother and baby were protected in the middle.

The elephants we followed down the hill

Another evening, near sunset, we came across a tower of giraffes. Their necks this time were not stiff and straight but supple and moving slowly from side to side and around, especially when close to another.

Their necks gently touching or nudging, then moving away or staying close and entwining with each other. Our guide said they were playing or practising their skills for another day when a fight might be underway. It was called necking and quite moving to watch.

Most people think warthogs are ugly animals, our guide told us. But the babies can be very cute and when you look at the adults again, they are not really ugly, just different. After returning to our tent one time and sitting out on the deck, a family of warthogs came past the path. Sue went inside to grab her video camera and I took off using my two walking sticks to take some photos. Sue wasn't far behind.

The adult warthogs knelt with their two front legs to eat whatever it was on the grass. Their long snouts had two small, upturned tusks at the end and their eyes were bulging in the middle of two pinned back long ears. Their legs were very short, but they still knelt for their mouths to get down low enough to eat off the ground. They had long tails with a bit of fluffiness at the end and their body on top looked disproportionately bigger over the tiny legs. We watched them as they stopped and grazed for a while and took photos. Sue left before me and went back to the tent.

'Aahh, eerrhh,' yelled Sue from inside, sounding suddenly frightened. Some odd noises followed. I rushed back (as fast as I could on two sticks) and at the sliding front door something fast and dark sped out past me. I followed the direction of movement and at the end of the deck near the bushes a small monkey looked up with a baby on her back. Then they disappeared into the bush.

I went inside and Sue was standing, shocked. 'Something just went whoosh straight past my face and over my head, so fast I didn't get to see what it was. I thought it might have been a bat or a flying fox. It was spread out as it flew past. Did you see it?'

'Yes, it was a monkey carrying a tiny baby.'

'Ooow, I missed seeing them.' Then Sue looked around. 'Look at the suitcase, these clothes and things weren't like this before. They have been going through them looking for something!'

'Did we go out and leave the door open?'

'I just came in to go to the loo and left the door slightly open for you. They must have squeezed in.'

'I remember one of the cleaning women saying to watch out for the monkeys. They like the sugar in the packets near the tea and coffee.'

'Yes, look, they have had a go over here, as well,' Sue added after walking to the table. 'That's incredible! A monkey!' We both laughed and shook our heads.

That's the only time we saw monkeys at Shamwari. They must have been watching the door so closely. Invisible to us outside in the trees.

But we saw plenty of other animals. The Plains Zebras kept running away whenever we came anywhere close, a Black Rhinoceros was often eating on the road and ignored us, the African buffalos performed a few jousting games in front of our eyes and the members of the African deer family (the Eland, Impala, Kudu and Springbok) sped past us so fast it was hard to distinguish what kind one was.

The countryside around Shamwari looked a lot like parts of Australia in some places. There were even some gumtrees along a main dirt road that the guide used as a landmark. He said they were considered an invasive tree in South Africa and disliked. Otherwise there weren't many tall trees to see, just a lot of low bush, dirt, a few water holes and one river. The game reserve's $250km^2$ had been several farms, and the land was being rehabilitated back to its wild native state.

Our tented accommodation and lodge at Shamwari (one of the six places to stay on the reserve) was modest, not showy or opulent. I don't think we could have stayed in a place that was too over the top. Lunch was served outside on the deck, while they served breakfast and dinner inside a two-level building with a kitchen at the back.

My accessible route to reception on the scooter went through doors on a path behind the kitchen. The entry side to the lodge after reception was down steps to raised decking with a small swimming pool near the lounge and an extension out into the bush, with umbrellas over tables and chairs. From our tented accommodation side, there was an accessible ramp down to the deck and lounge area.

It was boiling hot in the daytime, going over 30°C each day in December when we were there. We needed the umbrellas. Inside the lodge there was a lounge area downstairs and via a few steps, a dining room upstairs, with an open fireplace. Nights were cold, 12°C. The lounge area was a comfortable place to meet before a safari drive or just sit in, with reading material, drinks and snacks on hand.

After lunch one day, sitting out at a table under the umbrellas, looking over the water hole to the hills around, we chatted with one waiter. He was a tall, slim, dark Xhosa man in his early twenties, nicely attired and well trained. We enjoyed talking with him and hearing about how his people talked with clicks. But fairly quickly he didn't understand something we said. After we explained whatever we said that was odd, he burst out laughing and ran off, still laughing. When he came back, he asked us to tell him some more odd Australian words. We obliged, especially Sue recalling some of her father's Australian slang. Each word Sue told him ended up the same way. He thought they were hilarious and had to run off to contain his laughter each time. Things like – ridgy-didge (genuine), joe blakes (snakes) and snags (sausages) or furphy (a rumour or absurd story).

On our fourth and last day, Sue and I were the only people with our safari guide. It was early morning, and he drove us in the opposite direction to previous days. 'I thought I'd take you up the mountain a little way. It's misty and quiet. We might see some different things and it should be good for photography too.'

Soon we were passing through a mist with the finest of water droplets in the air. It was enough to dampen our clothing but not enough to need a covering; foggy enough to only see immediately in front of us and not much beyond. The mountainside road led to a plateau where there were some old buildings-crumbling remnants of a stone farmhouse and a small bell tower outside a just standing wooden building. Old pasture and farmland still evident. Mist wafted up and around, then settled. It was a beautiful scene of greys and muted brown-beige. The guide took a few photos and so did I. No need for an added mist lens for the effect; it was naturally there.

Further along the plateau, the guide parked the jeep near some low bushes and rocks. We sat and looked around silently. Then we saw movement in the fine cloudy mist. It was more than just the mist moving. Parts of figures began to gradually materialise. Several lions were lying together around the bush occasionally moving their heads. Some lions wandered off. Their creamy beige colours blended into the surrounds.

As we watched them our guide's look was intent on one female to our right lying down.

A lion in the mist

Then the lion moved a little. As she extended her back legs, he quickly told us to pay attention. Then suddenly as the lion finished extending her legs and bent her back, our guide said that was the signal to show she was about to race towards us. He picked up his gun in one hand and with the other hand pointed a finger directly at the advancing lion and with his eyes fixed on hers shouted loudly, 'No, no, no! Don't you even think about it. No!'

The lion stopped as our guide still had his finger pointed straight at her face. He told us she might have been going for the tyres. They enjoyed tearing at tyre rubber and had made their mark before. We wouldn't be going too far with mangled tyres, I thought. And then what would happen? But the lion stopped advancing.

We drove off and away to a more open and less misty area. After driving around the old property and down into a gully, our guide looked back and said he saw the lions moving along the road we had just taken.

'We'll go back and see what they are up to.' I had complete trust and didn't bat an eyelid.

Back up closer to the group there were several families, maybe nine lions in all. We made our way over to the side and watched them walk past along the road. Two of the older lions were sisters and some of the younger ones were like teenagers, the guide explained. There were no cubs or big manes about. Another older lion had left and was already a long way off in the distance, perhaps hunting. These lions were all just slowly moseying along in the rear.

We left the area after they went past and returned to the lodge for lunch.

They were four spectacular days with wild animals, and we felt immensely privileged to have been there. Able to sit for hours amongst those animals and watch them with their actions interpreted is something I will never forget.

The last thing we wanted to do before leaving Shamwari was to visit one of the Born Free Foundation areas on the game reserve. Our request was granted and on the last afternoon we were taken on a long drive to the other end of the game reserve.

I used my walking sticks to walk the short distance into the centre and passed a plaque dated September 1990 saying this Born Free Foundation Rescue and Education Centre at Shamwari is in memory of Julie Ward... whose life was cut short in Kenya at the age of 28. Julie Ward was a British photographer who loved Africa and its wild animals, and whose murder investigation had an unsatisfactory end.

Inside, the information hut we met a guide who explained the place to us. The hut was set up as a wildlife education centre with posters, seats and learning materials. We read from a big poster that the foundation is an animal charity, passionate about wild animal welfare. The guide also took us outside to see some animals living there. Sue and I were the only ones visiting the animals rescued from captivity and reading their stories of abuse was heartbreaking. I could only walk so far up the hill in the heat, but we had seen enough, anyway.

We left Shamwari Private Game Reserve the next day for Port Elizabeth to fly to Cape Town.

The twenty-kilometre drive from Cape Town International airport to our hotel in the city went past a vast collection of makeshift dwellings that I had only seen the likes of on TV news. The cobbled together housing made from bits of timber, tin, scrap metal, clothing material and all sorts of other odd pieces were assembled to provide some kind of shelter. The area looked a shanty town, a ghetto or a slum until I learned the country's name for it of 'township'. It was enormous and seemed to take forever to go past with more than a million people living there. I'd never seen or been so close to such a place in real life before. It was confronting and made me feel sad for the people living there and for the country that this had to be.

I didn't understand and couldn't comprehend what life might be like in the fifty odd townships in South Africa. Others I saw later stretched for kilometres beside the road. It seemed wrong driving past them and not helping. I usually photographed just about everything I saw on a trip away, but I couldn't lift my camera. I felt it would be even more wrong.

We were told they were largely black townships, and I was surprised to read later there are tours of the townships that have museums, theatres, shops, memorials and cafes. The contrast was even more jolting when I saw the substantial homes in Cape Town with barbed wire, electrified fencing and security cameras everywhere.

At our city hotel the next day, we went to the breakfast dining area where I used my scooter to get there because of the distance.

'Good morning. Welcome, come this way,' said a tall, well-dressed woman. The maître d' with great presence, confidence and authority led us through several rooms where diners were seated. The scene was an international one with people who looked as if they came from every country on earth. Their clothes were different, and some people looked exotic with their bright colours, headgear and large jewellery. The maître d' fitted the scene too, with her looks and manner. She had olive skin and I couldn't pick her ancestry. Perhaps it was Egyptian or Arabic or northern African or eastern European. I felt I was truly in a foreign place.

Adding to the exoticness of it all was the array of foods on display in the last room where our table was. Shortly after being seated our maître d' asked, 'What kind of coffee or tea would you like?' and then promptly followed with, 'We prepare dishes freshly cooked too. Your waiter will be here shortly', lifting her head and gently nodding to one nearby. 'What would you like first?' We ordered two double espressos in regular cups with hot water on the side and she disappeared.

I parked my scooter near the table and walked around the buffet tables, looking at what was on offer. There were many tables to go past with more in the next room. I have never seen such a variety of food choices that looked like they were from every country in the world too. So many kinds out on display and constantly being replenished. It was dazzling.

Linen tablecloths, silver service and palms in pots sat on carpeted floor surrounded by colonial glass windows of white timber looking out to the harbour with sun streaming in. We had a slow breakfast, very happy with the choices and just watching the surrounding people.

On the second morning the maître d' greeted us warmly and asked immediately if we were happy to have the double espressos again, leading us past the grand piano being played, closer to the window with views to the top of Table Mountain. After I sat down and looked up again through the windows to my left, I saw a very large cruise ship moored directly at the entry into the hotel.

The ship moored at the hotel front door

I was agasp. It was The World ship sitting there that sails around the world with its owners in rooms and apartments on board. On the right was Table Mountain, covered in cloud above the city buildings. Later, on a walk, we saw seals in the harbour happily playing around the cruise ship. What a place Cape Town was!

However, there was a severe water shortage. Signs were everywhere. *Cape Town is experiencing an extremely severe drought* and *Due to the increasing water shortage in the western cape please be conscious of your water usage and use it sparingly.*

In our hotel room the signs were more explicit – *Don't Rush to Flush. Please make use of the toilet neutraliser provided.* A blue spray bottle labelled as a no flush toilet water neutraliser sat on top of the cistern. Next to the toilet another sign read. *If it is yellow, let it mellow. If it's brown flush it down.* Signs also informed us that the water used to flush toilets was grey water collected from kitchens and some rooms then treated through the grey water collection system.

And there were more signs next to the bath, *Save Water, Shower Instead* and *Your bathplug has been removed, please contact our Duty Manager to arrange a bath pack.* And beside the bed, *Linen changed every fourth day.*

Apparently, rain hadn't fallen in years. We drank bottled water from some other country and didn't flush the toilets until absolutely necessary and used the spray. Handwashing was with alcohol sanitisers and paper napkins were 100% biodegradable.

The hotel was one of many in the Victoria and Alfred (or V&A) waterfront area. Security was everywhere. I didn't see any police, but security officers were aplenty guarding and patrolling shops and shopping centres. Feeling concerned, we didn't walk away from tourist areas.

While in Cape Town, we caught a taxi from the hotel to Kirstenbosch National Botanical Garden. In late December the main flowering season had passed and given the drought, it was also very dry. However, I loved seeing the yellow Bird of Paradise flower, developed and named in honour of Nelson Mandela-strelitzia reginae 'Mandela's Gold' and the pink fluffy Pompon tree in full flower. I had not seen either before.

Luckily, the cloudy weather cleared the day we went in the cable car up to the top of Table Mountain. A disabled persons assistant spotted me as soon as I arrived and showed us the fast way via a lift to avoid the long queues and put us at the front of any line. The ride up and down in the cable car was up a steep slope, almost vertical, with outstanding views along the way. The area at the top has accessible paths, easy for my scooter, and I could see out and down in all directions to the ocean, beaches, mountains, suburbs and the city.

After about a week exploring the city and the nearby regions – south to the Cape of Good Hope and east to the wine region of Stellenbosch, we boarded a cruise ship.

The cruise at the time was unique, sailing from Cape Town to Cape Town, covering both the west and east coasts of the southern part of Africa.

Shortly after boarding, the captain announced a change to our scheduled route. There was a severe weather warning for waters around Lüderitz, Namibia on the west coast for the next few days. We were not leaving but staying another day in Cape Town before going directly to our second scheduled stop of Walvis Bay, much further north in Namibia.

Sailing out the next afternoon, we looked back to the city of Cape Town with the flat-topped Table Mountain and adjacent mountain range behind it, standing out long after we departed. We sailed past the former prison on Robben Island, heading north west.

Christmas Day in Walvis Bay had a real ring to it in 2018. I expected a traditional Xmas lunch in the main dining room on board the ship. However, everything British about the Christmas lunch we'd been brought up with in Australia was missing aboard this mostly American passengered ship. No traditional roast pork with apple sauce, glazed ham, turkey with cranberry sauce with baked vegetables as a main or Christmas pudding with brandy custard for dessert. There was no Christmas lunch in the main dining room where only dinner at night was served. Some turkey was included on the menu that night, but it just didn't feel like Christmas.

On Boxing Day, we went on an off-road excursion into the Namib desert to see a moonscape created in a wind-worn valley plus an odd looking 1,000-year-old welwitschia plant in a desert that barely looked alive and one of the high sand dunes in the area.

When the ship departed the next day, we sailed close to the coast watching the long line of sand dunes extending south and coming out to meet the Atlantic Ocean waves.

After going around the Cape of Good Hope to the east coast there were safari drive excursions to game parks from most of the ports of call.

Those excursions were in busloads to travel the distance to get to the game reserve where about twenty people loaded onto several large safari vehicles with sometimes four persons seated across. It was hard to see any animals because the vehicle was so packed with people and because there were no animals about when we were there in the middle of the day. With a number of vehicles out at the same time, any animals we saw were soon frightened off. Some people didn't follow instructions-standing up to take photos and occasionally shouting or talking loudly.

We were pleased we went to Shamwari Game Reserve first before going on other game drives. Being able to sit quietly in a small-medium sized jeep with only a few other people and watch the animals for a significant period, with not just a quick look rushing past, had been wonderful. We knew how good the experience could be and how we had been spoilt.

At the end of one unsatisfying safari drive excursion, we went to the dining area at the game reserve for lunch. I was exhausted from walking in the heat from the vehicle (the scooter could only go so far), slow to arrive, and found nowhere to sit. Sue had gone off to try to find somewhere, and I leaned against a wall for support. One of the tourist guides spotted me and came to help. She found an empty seat at a table for four with two seated and asked if I could sit there. After they said yes, I almost fell onto the seat, feeling hardly able to move. I just wanted to sit, cool down and recover while Sue went off to the buffet to get some food.

'Country fare I'd call it here, not great,' the man with an American accent said to his wife unhappily just after I sat down.

How unfair and condescending, I thought. The food choices looked good to me as I went past.

I loved the movie *Annie Hall* for many reasons but one segment always stood out-the conversation between Woody Allen and Diane Keaton, outside on a balcony one night, where they are speaking to each other but thinking something else and what they are thinking appears as a caption in a cloud above their heads. When I was seated, I started my own internal monologue.

He jumped at me next, with a question.

'Is the food in your country as boring as in England? It's so tasteless. Do you have any decent food? What do you call the style of food served in your country?' I guessed he could tell I was Australian by how I said 'thank you' before sitting down.

'Modern Australian,' I answered. I didn't want to have more of a conversation with this man. I didn't like him. I hoped that answer would shut him up.

'Give me examples, tell me what decent food you have.'

Awful man. I didn't feel like explaining our great Australian food to him.

Emotional lability is one of the symptoms of multiple sclerosis (MS) as is easy fatigue both mentally and physically, especially with heat and after exercise. There is also difficulty with the speed of thinking and finding the right word. And I can get impatient, anyway. Whatever, he pressed my button. I wouldn't call it a tirade, although by then I had become irritated by a few passengers on the cruise. There were some very arrogant, rude people aboard.

I don't like a lot of North American food. I think it's terrible. That's what I wanted to say. Think of something awful and throw that back, I thought. That might shut him up. I just wanted to sit there, cool down and recover, undisturbed.

I think I had a short rave about how terrible I thought American food was, especially when ketchup and mayonnaise was added to just about everything.

To which he replied, 'I think ketchup goes with everything. I don't think you should eat anything without ketchup. In New York, I never do.'

This wasn't going anywhere pleasant. I just wanted him to keep quiet and let me be. What could I do to turn him off?

'What about that soft drink there?' I said, indicating the can in front of him he was drinking from. 'It's full of terrible things.'

Soft drink is so bad for your health—full of sugar, additives. How could you be drinking that?

Things were getting heated. He wanted me to justify my stance. I told him to read the label on the can. While he was reading and not talking, I got a needed break.

Great, now he's quiet.

Sue had been away getting some food from the buffet for both of us and suddenly arrived back.

He started again, holding the can. 'There's nothing wrong here.' How could he not see?

'Are you a doctor?' I asked him.

'Me? No.'

'Well, I am.'

Sue jumped in 'Maureen!' surprised at how I blurted it out so abruptly, not understanding what was happening. If there was anything logical happening, anyway.

I just wanted this to stop. I don't want to talk to this man anymore. Finally, I said, 'Could you please just let me have my lunch in peace?'

'You were the one who told me to read the label.' He said glaring. His wife (who was also away for most of the conversation) got up and made to leave.

'Have a nice cruise,' she said to me. He got up and left with her. Poor Sue didn't know what to think.

Thank goodness he was gone.

I saw him twice on the ship after that. Once when he was telling the captain off and the other when he passed me in a common area.

'Lovely to see you' he said, and I just waved with a nod.

The scheduled ports of call going up the South African east coast included Port Elizabeth, East London and Durban, before cruising the Indian Ocean on the way to Mozambique. In that country there was just the one stop in Maputo. I had started my malaria prevention tablets and read we should prepare ourselves to visit a very poor place with limited facilities.

However, a storm hit us after leaving Durban and we had to take shelter. The captain announced permission had been refused to dock at several ports. We went into a protected bay, moored offshore and waited.

The next day the captain announced the weather would not permit us to continue to Maputo, our last northerly port, and instead we would turn around, and start our route back to Cape Town. Somewhere in that time was New Year's Day and the beginning of 2019.

After stops in Richards Bay and Mossel Bay, we were back in Cape Town and travelled past the township area once more on our way to the airport to fly home.

On the plane from Cape Town, sitting in a window seat, I'd been looking out at the countryside and then looked away for a while. When we were soon to land in Johannesburg, I looked back out again and suddenly the redness was striking. The size and colour of the sun hit me. I had never seen a sunset with that post-box red colour before, nor one so big or so perfectly round. I loved sunsets and sunrises for their colour and the effect they have on their surrounds. But the ones I'd seen anywhere in the world were orange-yellow-red with flashes coming out from a rough circle. Not red red like this one and not a perfect circle. I recalled seeing photos of African sunsets in magazines, and I thought they must have been photoshopped. But they do exist, and this was a true African sunset like nowhere else in the world.

After a change of plane in Johannesburg we flew to Perth, from where we had left Australia, and waited for another plane to Melbourne. The three flights with waiting times made it a long day, leaving plenty of time to think.

I would love to repeat some of my African confrontations. Many were exciting new experiences. Others less so. But what a privilege to spend time with those African wild animals.

14. A FLOWER PARK IN JAPAN (2019)

We were at the Hitachi Seaside Park on an excursion during one of Japan's busiest holiday seasons. A mass of people and blue flowers wove together on the hillsides, and I'd never seen anything like it.

Our ship arrived at the port of Hitachinaka, to the glee of the locals who came out to see the first international cruise ship to berth there. The port, just north of Tokyo, was a replacement for the usual stop at nearby Oarai.

On an early Sunday morning, the dockside area already had several marquees and market stalls out. Two large canvas shade cloths were high over long tables with chairs arranged for dining. Some tents with blue and white striped pointed tops stood out at the back and red carpets were down in front with microphones on stands and a band to one side setting up. A small group of people waiting near the end of the ship's gangway, behind fencing, were waving to us and taking photographs–photographs with themselves in the foreground, of us, of the ship, of everything happening, happily chatting in Japanese. Passengers waved back. Some children dressed in school uniform held a sign saying Welcome to Ibaraki (the prefecture). We disembarked into the merry throng to board a bus leaving on the flower park excursion.

The extended holiday season of Golden Week in late April, early May 2019 coincided with even more holidays granted for the crowning of a new emperor. Everyone had time off and when we arrived at the park on a beautiful sunny day, most of Japan seemed to be there.

The seasonal plantings at the popular park beside the sea ensured something spectacular was always on show. In Spring, the park's hills are covered in the gentle flow of four-and-a-half million pale blue

Nemophila flowers, while in autumn, the mounds of thirty-two thousand Kochia bushes turn a glorious crimson.

Nemophila have delicate, cup-shaped flowers of five petals and most species include the phrase 'baby blue eyes' in their common name because of their sky-blue colour. The small, low-growing plants love the sun and being crowded together.

The scene from a distance was daunting at first because the flowers weren't the only things close together. The immense crowd made me doubt that I would be able to move up the steep hill, and I wasn't sure if my scooter would make it to the top, but the smooth concrete path wound around the beds of flowers at a manageable incline and was wide enough for two people. The Japanese people who passed us were courteous, orderly and considerate. Not a problem. To take photos, they stepped to one side and kept behind the cordoning rope. I joined them when I couldn't stop myself from taking even more photos.

I moved along and around the corners of the path up the hill at the same pace as the crowd and Sue was close by. Siting on my scooter, the scene of the flowers and people merged into one.

The best view came after we arrived at the top. Looking out, the crowd snaked their way up and down the hills and looked like they were trunks and branches of a blue tree. Up there, I could also see the full extent of the enormous park adorned with waves of blue flowers situated beside the North Pacific Ocean. We could even see our ship moored in the distance.

The scooter handled the descent better as we travelled the longer, less-steep side of the hill which was still filled with crowds. The view back from the bottom was like another world, with the crowd surging upward.

View looking back up the hill of Nemophila flowers

At the base of the hill, the surrounding scene was a stark contrast to the one we left. Although there were more people standing or lying down taking photos of the flowers, it was the actions of others I found extraordinary.

Small dogs were dressed up, carried in baskets, pushed in prams or arranged in front of flowers or signs for photographs. Couples and singles had dogs – special, odd, all kinds. Dogs of the same breed seemed to gather in specific areas and were having collective photos taken. Sometimes, one or two of the dogs weren't interested in sitting or standing still and moved away to the laughter of their owners. Patience and persistence prevailed, no matter how long it took.

Other groups had spread rugs out to the side of walkways for picnics, and the people attending were dressed up for the occasion. There were a few food vans and ice cream stalls, but most people had brought their own food arranged neatly in containers. Families sat under trees for shade or tiny tents for extra protection. This was an event for everyone.

People queued in orderly lines in front of official park signs where professional photographers took photos while others used their own cameras. The cameras varied between the large, small, long, and those with multiple lenses, held by hand or on tripods. The Nemophila flowing up the hills were shot at different angles and depths. Some people were so close to a flower they could have eaten it. But manners would have prevailed, I'm sure.

Everyone was merry. Only a few people seemed to be not of Japanese heritage. All in harmony, or 'Wa'-the Japanese cultural concept of peaceful unity and conformity within a group, enjoying being together rather than alone.

We happily wandered along the gravel paths to the Nemophila entrance through the kind of crowd we'd never seen before.

Many areas of the park are worth exploring, such as the ones with many different species of tulips, but time was limited. We returned to the blue hills where the trolley cars were ready to take people around the park and bicycles were out for rent.

The long walk from there to the main entrance of the park was a few kilometres. At the halfway point, an enormous banner hung over us showing one huge Nemophila flower and an arrow pointing the way to the hilly fields. I stopped to take a photograph to remember what flower it was and how to spell the name.

When we booked the excursion, we didn't know that Nemophila flowers would be on display. The ship tours' name, 'Seaside Park and Fish Market' gave no indication. I'd never seen a Nemophila flower, let alone rolling hillsides of them.

We went back to the bus, leaving the crowds, flowers, and the dogs still coming and going.

Before returning to the ship, we stopped at the Nakaminato Fish Market. This large, regional market was also exciting. The oysters were the size of small dinner plates and the sardines, filleted and split, spun in a circle on a makeshift, A-framed machine, drying. Some areas inside were difficult to get into on my scooter, but I saw many sea creatures I'd never seen before out on display.

After not long enough there either, we returned to the ship and found more to look at on the pier before boarding. There was a crowd of people and activity everywhere.

Local schools had what looked like dancing competitions underway and young girls, arranged in groups with teachers, were wearing matching brightly coloured dresses. Ones with pleated skirts sewn on below the waist. They took turns to come onto the big red-carpet square. Parents and family of the small children were seated in rows five deep facing the square. Groups of children came onto the carpet stage in turns. They organized themselves in lines - four across and four deep and stood waiting for the music to start.

The music was different for each group, and the routines they performed were different too. They held sticks in their hands with coloured ribbons at the end and were moving them around as well as their bodies. Some of the little ones were still learning, turning the wrong way and the smiles on people's faces watching (especially the ship's passengers) was only just stifling loving laughter.

The market stalls behind the performing area and its spectators were selling gifts, books, sweets, cakes, cooked foods and pickled vegetables. At an information booth, I asked about the region and other places to visit. Communicating was difficult and by the time I left with a few brochures we were mostly just smiling and bowing to each other.

A few people were wandering around dressed as movie characters posing for photos while farm machinery was also out on show. Everything was set out on a level, even surface and going around on my scooter was easy. It was some event, and I still don't know its name or what it was about. Could it have been just for us?

Sailing away that night, my thoughts were full of wonder at all things unique to Japan.

15. VACCINES AND GARDENS (2019)

I was in the basement of a city building in Vancouver awaiting my first dose of Shingrix. At the time, this vaccine was not available in Australia but supplied widely in the United States and Canada. No matter how hard I tried to find out when it would be available in Australia, I hit a brick wall. However, the vaccination clinic in Canada agreed immediately. Let me rewind and explain how I came to be there.

By late 2017, I really needed a vaccination to prevent the shingles disease or Herpes Zoster. Both my neurologist and general practitioner (GP) were urging me. 'It is not nice to have shingles and you are more likely to get it with your treatments for multiple sclerosis (MS) and your older age.'

I kept saying, 'But Zoster Vax is a live vaccine, and I can't have it, remember?'

I didn't want to take the risk (even if it was low) of developing an overwhelming infection because I was immunocompromised. I had read about some devastating cases.

We usually try to have one overseas trip booked in advance. Much earlier, as soon as I saw a cruise from Tokyo to Vancouver via Alaska, we booked it. However, that cruise line refused to allow my mobility scooter on board, no matter how hard we tried. When our travel agent told my story to another cruise line, they immediately invited me aboard their next cruise sailing the same route. The cruise included a stop in Kamchatka, Russia, and sailed over the North Pacific Ocean before sailing down the coast of Alaska, entering the Inside Passage to Vancouver. It sounded wonderful and we booked it. So luckily, I was going to be in Canada in May 2019.

Shingrix requires two doses, two to six months apart. While I had the first dose sorted out, I didn't know where I would have the second. If I had to go back to Canada for the second dose, it would be worth it. Besides, I liked Canada.

I first visited Canada when I was a medical student on a gap term working at a hospital in Saskatoon, Saskatchewan in the prairies. I travelled on my own, mostly by rail, from Vancouver to Montreal, enjoying the sights and experiences. I enjoy Canada and would easily go again.

In 2019, Sue and I were in Vancouver for one night and two days. The ship arrived early on a Thursday morning, and we were leaving on a direct flight late the next night. The clinic had appointments on Friday and the timing worked out well.

Vancouver harbour's cruise ship terminal is right in the city's heart, flanked by a floatplane terminal on one side and a train station on the other. Across the road from where our ship docked are hotels and footpaths leading into the city.

The train station includes Sea Bus and SkyTrain services. The building is the same outside as when it was constructed in 1914, in the heyday of rail travel across Canada. The station was called the Canadian Pacific Railway building when I was first there, the start to the transcontinental route. It has changed a lot after becoming the Waterfront Station. At footpath level, it blends in with the surrounding city buildings and its architecture is lost. It wasn't until I looked down from a footbridge that I saw the building in its true grandness. I'd been on the SkyTrain from there to the airport more than once in recent years, but it wasn't until I was up high that I recognised the building.

We decided to visit the famous Chinese garden because I'd never been there before. But as we neared the area close to the garden, the city changed, and I felt uncomfortable. It was unusual because I'd never felt unsafe in Canada before. We almost turned around to go back.

I learned that Downtown East Side, near Chinatown, is thought to be the worst area in Vancouver. Apparently, drug dealers and addicts live and hang out there.

We noticed people did look rather different, and some looked at us in disturbing ways. We hurried down the street to the gardens where small tourist buses were parked outside.

We went into the Dr Sun Yat-Sen park first, beside the Classical Chinese Garden. A large bust of the doctor was stationed at the park's entrance. I read he was the father of modern China and the first president of the Republic of China. He had visited Vancouver several times to raise funds for the nationalist movement.

The winding paths inside the park were easy to navigate on my scooter. The shrubs and bamboo had been carefully chosen and the paths lead to a pagoda to rest in. I felt tranquil amongst the carefully placed rocks and plants and the waterlily-covered pond. The pond links the park and the classical garden.

But I couldn't go into the Dr Sun Yat-Sen Classical Chinese Garden because each entry was blocked with raised dividers to step over. The Garden, with its principles of Taoism and Feng Shui, craggy rocks, ponds and delicate foliage, would have to wait until I could walk with my cane. Unfortunately, we did not have enough time that day.

We took a different route, past other older buildings, back to our hotel at the harbour waterfront area.

Earlier in the year, I sent a few emails to the Travel Medicine and Vaccination Centre in Vancouver. The best clinic for me was on Burrard Street, close to where the ship docked at Canada Place and our hotel. It was only a ten-minute walk.

Until this point, I had assumed the clinic would be accessible via scooter and didn't check until the day before the appointment after I received a message to confirm the booking. When I asked about access, they told me there were renovations underway blocking all but one staircase. I'd forgotten about the shopping centres under office blocks in Canada and how some were only accessible by stairs. Thankfully, they gave me another route.

When we walked and scootered through the city to the clinic the next day, the streets were mostly empty. I will always remember walking outside in the snow, with few people about, during my first visit to Canada, in Montreal. To my surprise when I opened a building's glass door, I saw crowds inside an enormous open space with floors of shops all around and a train arriving at a station in the middle below me! Many years later I was similarly intrigued when I discovered Montreal's invisible underground city extending kilometres between buildings. It wasn't snowing, or cold then and seemed to be the preferred way for people to move about. I wondered if that was where the crowds were in Vancouver.

We went into the building next door, found the lift and went down one level. The instructions after that were complicated: *turn left after exiting the lift and open a door marked 'No Entry'*. There were more lefts and rights and corridors and paths before we finally reached a door with a sign, 'No Access'. After opening the door carefully, I found myself in a small shopping complex. Most shops were closed for renovations, but the small clinic was open behind a glass shopfront.

I rode my scooter into a tight space with four seats around a reception desk and an adjacent treatment room.

Two people were chatting, waiting after their vaccinations. A nurse called me and explained a doctor read my application and approved the Shingrix. I'd forgotten my yellow book to record the vaccination and after I received the injection, she wrote the batch number on a card to insert later. First dose done.

After the vaccination, we went to the nearby historic Anglican Christ Church Cathedral. Over the years, I'd walked past admiring its Gothic Revival architecture from the outside. But, with no ramp and only stairs, I couldn't get inside. We went shopping instead.

We didn't find an underground city, but did find larger linking shopping malls below ground, all suitable for my scooter.

Later that night we caught the SkyTrain to the airport.

Back home I told my GP I had received the first dose of Shingrix and was trying to organise the second but hoped it might become available in Australia in the meantime.

In the following months, Shingrix became available in other countries within the European Union (EU) but not Australia. I thought about the United Kingdom, but Canada was closer.

In September, we were meeting with friends and holidaying in Switzerland and Sicily. Switzerland is not part of the EU, so I had no luck there. Sicily, being part of Italy, is part of the EU. However, my emails to Palermo and elsewhere in Sicily went unanswered.

Then I had the bright idea of trying Singapore. We were stopping there for a night to rest and to visit the Botanic Gardens, anyway. Whilst not in North America or the EU, from my experience and knowledge about Singapore, it seemed likely they could get anything.

I Googled Travel Medicine and Vaccination Clinic Singapore and the medical centre attached to the Tan Tock Seng Hospital came up: The Traveller's Health and Vaccination Clinic.

The hospital is one of the largest multi-disciplinary hospitals in Singapore and is attached to one of the universities. Emails flowed quickly. They did not have Shingrix in stock all the time but given enough notice, it could be obtained. There was plenty of time to get Shingrix before October. I booked an appointment for the day we'd be there.

In Australia, the herpes zoster vaccine is free for anyone over the age of seventy, otherwise there is a cost. In Canada, they gave me Shingrix at the same price they would charge a Canadian. Whilst in Singapore, it seemed only available on specific request with clinical reasons, and at a much higher price.

Come October, five months after the first dose, we flew to Singapore.

I hadn't been far up the Singapore River and I wanted to walk along a section further away from where I'd been before. We arrived at our hotel, a good way up the river, in the early evening.

From the hotel, we had a marvellous view of the river flowing down to Marina Bay and the stunningly designed Marina Bay Sands Hotel. Three tall towers of the hotel are linked at the top by three acres of park, with swimming pools and gardens stretching out over all of them. We were up there with my scooter a few years earlier. Beside the hotel, the wheel of the Singapore Flyer flashed with coloured lights and beyond the towers, scores of ships were waiting in Singapore Harbour.

The following day, we had time to walk part of the Singapore River Walk before my appointment. Scootering along flat level concrete was easy and although water flowing is always uplifting, our walk along the north side of the river was not as picturesque as I had imagined.

Apartment blocks, hotels, restaurants and shops, rising up, jumbled together, gave me a suffocating feeling. Our walk led us down to Robertson Quay, Clarke Quay and improved when we reached Boat Quay, where the river spread out, surrounds opened up and a different mood was in play. The scene across the river to the south side was of colourful historic shophouses close to the water with towering office skyscrapers shooting up behind them. The river was full of small boats moving and cruising back and forth.

Further along our walk, just before the Victoria Concert Hall, there is a statue of Tan Tock Seng, commemorating him with a plaque reading, [he] *arrived from Malaka in 1819*, [became a successful businessman] *but always gave back to the community, and his legacy is carried on in a temple and hospital that stand to this day.* The very hospital I was going to for my vaccination.

We caught a taxi there not long after, where the clinic at the Tan Tock Seng Hospital is on level 4 of the Medical Centre Block. I parked my scooter beside a group of lounges in a large central waiting area with treatment rooms in a square surrounding it. There was a familiar western style to the setting, and I remembered British rule only ended in the 1960s.

The doctor I saw was a professor of infectious diseases. His name and the way he spoke suggested he also had some British background. He was taken aback by my World Health Organisation International Certificates of Vaccination booklet – my yellow book. He said he hadn't seen one like it in many years and the handwriting on the cover was immaculate. It was the original from my first vaccination in September 1976 before travelling overseas. It seemed I was once a neat writer. We chatted for a while before I saw the nurse and had my second dose of Shingrix.

Sue and I were then free to spend the rest of the afternoon in the Singapore Botanic Gardens. Singapore is proud the 160-year-old garden was the first UNESCO World Heritage Site in Singapore and the only tropical botanic garden on the list. It was hot and humid where the taxi dropped us off and we moved quickly to a more open area in the extensive 82-hectare site.

After diverting along the Heliconia Walk, keeping an eye out for colourful sunbirds, we arrived at the National Orchid Garden and didn't go beyond there.

We loved seeing the orchid display of over 1,000 species and 2,000 hybrids. The artistic way the orchids were arranged was special, with different colours and sizes, grouped and stacked on rocky platforms and walls, and so pleasing to the eye. I especially loved the scene they created on top of several archways over one path. The orchids were clustered together with green leaves uppermost and their yellow flowers hanging gently down.

Orchid arches in Singapore

Later that night, we flew to Zurich.

I'd had the full course of Shingrix, and the possibility of me getting shingles was now highly unlikely. Job done. Next adventure on.

16. THE SWISS CONCIERGE (2019)

After a gruff greeting at the hotel in Switzerland, the concierge became the star. Initially, I mistook his desk for reception. With a 'Not so!' he pointed us in the right direction. I almost didn't go back to him for help the next day, but I am so glad we did.

We were on a Swiss rail trip that included a stopover in Interlaken, a beautiful town in the country's west. Most visitors go for the Jungfraujoch excursion, and I thought that's what we'd do. I went to the concierge for tickets and asked for advice about going with my scooter.

The historic Jungfrau Railway – the train to Jungfraujoch – goes through the Eiger mountain in the Bernese Alps to the highest train station in Europe. The views are supposed to be stunning, and a once-in-a-lifetime trip.

Another 'Not so!' The concierge explained, 'There will be so many tourists crowding everything out. You won't see anything. They'll be in front of the windows and squashed up to the railings at the lookout. The train is old, and I'm not sure if your scooter could get on.'

But he had another suggestion. 'Let me suggest a route that will show you the real Switzerland.'

He described a round-trip to the Schilthorn, up almost as high in the alps, and we were all ears.

I'd never heard of the Schilthorn but remembered the mountain peak where the villains were in the James Bond film *On Her Majesty's Secret Service*. That was one of Bond's most spectacular rescues. The concierge explained the route involved trains, cable cars, and a bus. I pointed out the many changes, but the concierge reassured me I would manage on my scooter and he seemed very proud to tell us about his country. He gave us the Swiss Skyline, Schilthorn Piz Gloria, Summer Guide 2019 pamphlet, which included a map and outlined the route. We were sold. Forget what we thought we would do.

We arrived at Interlaken West railway station from Zurich the night before. As we found our way to the hotel, I was unimpressed with the kitsch tourist shops and the crowds of visitors walking along Bahnhofstrasse.

The next day, we ventured in the opposite direction to Interlaken Ost railway station, hoping to see more traditional buildings. But there weren't any old buildings to see in that part of Interlaken either. At the station, we caught a Swiss Rail train to Lauterbrunnen to start our Schilthorn trip.

After getting off at Lauterbrunnen, we walked and scootered from the platform into the entrance of the aerial cableway going up the mountain. I couldn't believe how easy it was. The waiting cable car was accessible, and I rode in on my scooter, with only a few others. The short, scenic ride up over pine trees ended at Grütschalp and, once again, our next mode of transport – a train, was ahead. I found out later the Mürrenbahn cableway and rail are a linked hybrid system connecting Lauterbrunnen with Mürren, an isolated village in the mountains.

Two old train carriages with huge windows were waiting. Men with lifting devices stood ready to help. I rode onto a metal plate and a man cranked a lifter to move me higher, level with the carriage for an easy ride in. Others left the cable car for one of the many mountain hiking trails.

The mountain railway goes back and forth on a narrow-gauge, one-way rail line between Grütschalp and Mürren. We travelled along a mountain ridge, above sheer cliffs, and had glorious views of the valley below and snow-capped mountain ranges above it. The range's peaks were those of the Mönch, Jungfrau and Eiger mountains. Below the jagged folds of snow-covered rock, lower down the mountain, farmhouses and green pastures were scattered over ridges and slopes. The rail line was on its own mountain side and passed through lush meadows and forests. I thought it was an alpine symphony of sights.

The train stopped at the edge of Mürren. After looking at the map, I was worried about how we would find our way from the station through the town, to the next aerial cableway. But the concierge was correct, Mürren was a charming little place with good signage and an easy path to follow. The well-worn bitumen walking trail ran past alpine houses, a few small hotels and guest houses, and an occasional restaurant.

The concierge suggested we stop for lunch at one of the traditional eateries. We spotted two places where people sat at tables, covered in patterned tablecloths, enjoying themselves, but we continued walking.

As we strolled, the view became an extension of the glorious sights we saw before, and the Eiger mountain moved closer until it stood in front of us. The massive mountain is where over sixty climbers have died while attempting to climb the sheer walls of the steep north face. The face is thought to be one of the most challenging and dangerous ascents in the world and there it was in my face!

At the other end of Mürren, we reached another aerial cable station. After we showed our Swiss Travel Pass, they gave us a Schilthorn Piz Gloria ticket at no charge. I rode easily into the waiting cable car where there were signs advertising the Skyline Walk and the Thrill Walk higher up, at the next station of Birg.

We rose up into the mountains and left the green meadows and pastures. The cable car with glass windows moved over snow, ice, and rock on the steep climb up to the Birg platform, which sat at 2677 m. Once there, I rode out through the station to find people sitting on wooden benches close to the building. We went past them onto a wooden deck with bits of ice and snow at our feet.

The deck turned into transparent mesh flooring where in the spaces between the metal I could see and feel the drop straight down the mountain. This Skyline Walk extended out further over the drop with glass panels at the railing edge for an extra gasp effect. The word Jungfrau was inscribed on one section and a wall of mountains rose up in the distance. Jungfrau, at 4,158 m is one of the main summits of the Bernese Alps. There were magnificent views from the deck all-around of snow-covered mountain ranges.

After hearing shrills of laughter, I looked over the edge. People below walked around the cliff on narrow see-through-mesh steps and walkways leading to a tiny balcony. It was the new Thrill Walk.

I looked in awe, pleased to be sitting on my scooter over the transparent mesh. I felt less afraid of the height on the larger balcony, where I posed for a photo. The solid yellow base of my scooter stood out on the mesh below my black waterproof pants and a red wind-and-rain-proof jacket.

We could see the next cables going up further into the sky and every now and then, when the cloud cleared, we could see the summit of the Schilthorn. After we recovered from the thrills at Birg, we were keen to go higher and caught the next cable car to Bond World and the Schilthorn Piz Gloria. We ascended into clouds and past tall cable towers on steep slopes of snow. At the top I rode out easily again, with only a tiny gap between level surfaces, into the station. I immediately saw advertising for the 007 Walk of Fame show, which included all things Bond. But we wanted to go outside and see the view.

As soon as we were outside the 360-degree view of the many mountain peaks around us was breathtaking. But we had to be careful of the snow and ice on the concrete surface of the viewing deck. Sue almost slipped over a few times and I didn't want to get off and use my walking sticks with rubber tips until I was on a dry section.

People lined up for a photo, holding a Swiss flag with its white cross on a red background. They stood in front of a sign saying *2970m, Swiss Skyline, Eiger Mönch Jungfrau*. We lined up too and didn't have to wait long. Sue's bright purple Gortex jacket over black pants looked great with white snow behind as she held out the flag.

The names of the mountain peaks were written on signs attached to the railings around the viewing deck. But there were so many peaks and I found it hard to distinguish between them. As I went around in a circle on my scooter, I counted over 100. The mountains came and went as soft wispy clouds moved across, hiding some mountains and revealing others. Heavier clouds hung around snow covered ragged mountain ranges in the distance. We were above and also within white clouds with the thin ones clearing around us first to show the bright blue skies high up over the distant mountains.

Beside the station, there is a polygonal shaped building with glass panelled walls. Inside the three levels are restaurants, shops and places where *On Her Majesty's Secret Service* was filmed. Still more interested in being outside, we moved on.

The trip back down was also spectacular. The cable car descended into swirling cloud and going past a tower I recalled the villain's helicopter flying up. We seemed so close to snow at times it felt as if we were skiing our way down with Bond.

We changed cable cars at Birg, without more thrills, going lower, under the clouds and emerging where green appeared once more at Mürren with its pine trees and grasses.

From the Mürren cableway station, we went in a new direction, straight down. I looked out back up the mountain to see the buildings of Mürren sitting close together atop an enormous mound sticking out the side of a mountain, with cliffs at the edge. We returned to green pastures with views of snow-capped alps.

The Concierge recommended seeing Gimmelwald and it was the next stop on the descent. We got off and what a charming, little mountain village it is.

We walked through and saw only a few houses, and, between a wooden house and a barn, another mountain seemed to jump out at us. No one else was there. The collection of houses, a hostel, a hotel, and a Pensione ended after a five-minute walk from the cable car station. The views around of mountain scenery were sensational.

We spotted a sign for lunch outside an old, two-storey wooden chalet hotel and went into the rear garden with tables and chairs. As soon as I saw the view from the tables, I rode fast to the edge on my scooter and claimed a table with the best view. I needn't have rushed because no one else was looking. There were only two others there, already seated in another area.

The warm vegetable soup and crusty bread we ate were perfect while we sat marvelling at the view. Red geraniums popped out of pots hanging over the railing edge, with white ones further along. What a wonderful foreground for a photo I thought straight away. The mountain in front of us looked like a stretched-out circus tent with a white coating of snow at the top. Moss and alpine greens peeked out from the snow high up and became denser in a vertical drop as they merged into the forest below.

The table for lunch at Gimmelwald

Gimmelwald seemed to be *the* place for hikers. At lunch, I noticed a young man who looked like he'd just finished a steep climb. With his solid, well-worn walking boots, grey T-shirt, and damp crumpled shorts he looked as if he had been walking for days. He went into the Mountain Hostel just below us.

Satisfied, we walked slowly back to the cable car station, past gorgeous purple-red flowers. The hollyhocks were nestled in clumps alongside the gently sloping path down to the station.

I saw a sign back at Mürren showing the way to a funicular leading to a flower park and hiking trail at Allmendhubel. I have put that on my list to do another time if it has an accessible path.

We were the only people at the cable station. The woman at the ticket office wondered why we stopped there. She said people rarely got off because there was nothing there! We told her about our great lunch and the view, but she seemed unimpressed. I suppose she sees that scene all day, every day.

We caught the next cable car down on our final aerial link and fell gently down the cliffs in a dramatic descent into the Lauterbrunnen Valley, and the floor, at Stechelberg. Waterfalls, all with deep drops, flanked the cliffs along the valley leading back to the town of Lauterbrunnen.

The cable car station at Stechelberg is also the site of the local bus stop. There were more people there than we had seen all day. We joined the queue and others soon followed. By the time the bus came, there was a crowd and I wondered if we would all fit in.

Looking out from the bus stop, I could see a valley of green fields and farms. Looking up, I couldn't see the mountains above the sheer cliffs. They were a memory now. In a world of their own.

The driver of the yellow bus to Lauterbrunnen unfolded the ramp for me to ride in. Everyone fitted and we drove alongside a river, stopping at several bus stops along the way. The most spectacular waterfall we saw was Staubbachfall, which dropped a sheer 300m, close to the village.

We entered Lauterbrunnen and saw it properly for the first time. When we arrived at the station earlier in the day, the underground entrance to the aerial cableway was in front of us. There was no need to move further up the platform to go into the town.

Lauterbrunnen has a population of about 2,000 people, much bigger than the little rural places where we had just been. It seemed busy when we arrived, and the bus driver was not impressed when a minivan parked in his spot. Masses of tourists milled about, being picked up or dropped off. He blew his horn and hopped out to find the driver. Within a few minutes, the van was out of the way and we got off at the stop opposite the train station. I noted a bright yellow, red, black and white Swiss Post logo painted on the bus as I scootered out.

On the train trip back to Interlaken Ost, I saw wooden farmhouses, green pastures, and this time, cows wearing bells around their necks.

The whole area of the Bernese Alps is wonderful. It is also known as the German Alps. German is the primary language spoken, but everyone seemed to speak English well, and many other languages.

At the train station of Interlaken Ost, we arrived on the opposite side from where we had started in the morning and we noticed the water nearby. We soon realised a lake was close by. If we had time, we could have caught a ferry from the port, up the river and travelled around Lake Brienz. Every form of transport we'd encountered that day was seamlessly connected. Perfect for me on my scooter.

Interlaken, as the name suggests, lies between two lakes: Lake Thun and Lake Brienz. Both lakes are connected by a river running through the town, the River Aare. We had just discovered the waterways. While we had walked along the main road near the river, we had missed it altogether.

After crossing a bridge, we walked back to the hotel along the north side of the river. Walking along the promenade beside the River Aare, we noticed other people on either side, also out enjoying a walk.

In the late afternoon, with the fading sunlight peering through the trees, the river walk was lovely.

Further along, we crossed over the river and found our way to the hotel for a brief rest.

The hotel where we were staying had an Italian restaurant and a dining room with a special week of Thai dishes on offer. However, when we spoke to the concierge the day before, he told us about the local Swiss restaurants where we could experience real Swiss cooking. He gave us a map of Interlaken and marked where the two restaurants were.

The night before, we went to one restaurant called Bären, past the Interlaken West station. The restaurant was in a large wooden chalet that included an outdoor seating area and a one-room restaurant inside in a cosy, casual setting.

Sue looked at the menu offering mountain cuisine and saw Swiss fondues on offer but wasn't sure if ordering that was too touristy. She asked the waitress, who exclaimed, 'No, the locals have it all the time. We make proper ones, it's good.'

After the waitress explained the different types, Sue ordered the traditional one. I had fish from a nearby freshwater lake. Two great meal choices, we thought.

This night, we were keen to try the other restaurant. After our rest we were off.

We headed west but turned right in the middle of the tourist strip—full of watch shops and souvenirs—near the local information centre. The road led to the river and a bridge with walkways on either side of the road. As I scootered over, a historic-looking unusual structure caught my attention down the river. A long open gable roof with a timbered railing sat on a concrete structure. The old sluice gates controlled the flow of water between the lakes, one 2m higher than the other. I got off my scooter to stand up and admire it.

Looking up the river on the other side of the bridge, red geraniums and coloured pansies in boxes hung off a rail, signalling a change of scene. I looked straight ahead and saw the old town for the first time. The centuries old buildings, town square, public buildings, and low-rise houses had more geraniums spilling out of window boxes. A magnificent scene. Yes, this and the Schilthorn are the real Switzerland.

We entered a traditional town centre with Swiss buildings and locals. I looked at our map, and as well as the markings for the Stadthaus restaurant where we were headed, I noticed the concierge's marks outlining a walk around the old town. Thank goodness we found this part—Unterseen Altstadt, a sign said—of Interlaken. I would have been disappointed if we had missed it. One of my brothers, who had been to

Interlaken the year before, told me what a wonderful place it was. But, until then, I had no idea what he meant.

The Stadthaus is a bar, café, restaurant, hundreds of years old. It is also much larger than the Bären of the night before. The modernised interior has a bar running along one side of a big, open, square room full of tables and chairs. The concierge told us we might not be interested in some of the fast foods, such as burgers and chips, but they had many alpine classics; he was right again.

The restaurant served wines from Switzerland and regional beers on tap. We had already enjoyed very nice Swiss wines, so we tried the regional beers instead.

I don't recall exactly what we ate, but the meals were regional specialties, freshly made in the kitchen and delicious.

What a day! How did we fit so much in? We did not rush at any stage.

Our one-day round trip to the Schilthorn involved two Swiss Rail trains, seven aerial cable cars, one Bergbahn Lauterbrunnen-Mürren (BLM) narrow gauge mountain train, and one postal bus. The cost of each was included in our Swiss Travel Pass. Also included would have been a trip on the waiting ferry, if we'd chosen that. But there is a limit to just how much joy one can have in a day! All thanks to the star concierge.

17. SICILIAN SURPRISES (2019)

'Errh!' the much older woman, in a dark dress with a walking stick, called out from the other side of the road. Her voice was just audible above the noise of cars speeding past. I was sitting on my scooter with friends beside me trying to cross a main street using a pedestrian crossing in Siracusa (or Syracuse), Sicily. But the traffic wasn't stopping and there were no traffic lights. As soon as the woman had our attention she walked out onto the crossing, stopped, held up her walking stick and the cars stopped. She waved her hand at us to come forward and cross.

We obeyed. Once we were all on the other side the woman uttered, 'Sorry, sorry,' and shaking her head and stick at the traffic again, walked off.

Sicily was full of surprises. This one happened half-way through our trip, at Syracuse on the south-eastern side of the Italian island.

We started the trip a week before in Palermo, further west up on the north coast. Sue and I flew from Zurich at the end of a rail holiday in Switzerland. We met up with Robin, our ex-Aussie friend, arriving from London the same evening.

Robin said a friend told her she would only go to Palermo for two reasons—to see the Cappella Palatina (or Pallatine Chapel) and the Cattedrale di Monreale (or Monreale Cathedral). After some brief investigation, we all agreed, seeing them was the priority over our two days there.

It was a noisy first night with interrupted sleep from the sound of a man talking loudly from his food van parked outside. Motorbikes came and went until the early hours of the morning, making more noise in the slightly widened area on our narrow back street.

In daylight the next morning, as soon as we were out the front door, the sight of rubbish all over the place was striking. The paper, plastics and food scraps were not just in our street but also in other areas as we walked through the city. Garbage bags lay overflowing and looked like they had been there for too long. The discarded items even lay in front of centuries old historic buildings. It was hot and dirty with me on my scooter dodging rubbish, on the way to the Pallatine Chapel.

Our route along Via Maqueda and Corso Vittorio Emanuele was part of a historic walk through the old city. Tourists were everywhere and locals were calling out, touting souvenirs, food and other goods for sale. As we walked along the pedestrian only promenades, with a multi-language babble humming around us, people walked past and through our party of three. We had to concentrate so as not to get lost.

We arrived at the Royal Palace too late to see the chapel. It was a Sunday morning and only open for a short time.

'Let's go to Monreale then?' I suggested. 'Come back and see the chapel tomorrow.' Everyone agreed.

The town of Monreale is out of the city on a hill and not within walking distance. We thought we would go by bus and went to nearby Piazza Indipendenza to catch one.

We were unfamiliar with the public transport system and must have looked apprehensive near the bus stop. Soon a man walked up, asked where we wanted to go and offered to drive us. People rarely do that when I'm on my scooter, considering it a load and a problem. The man told us if we caught the bus it would stop at the base of a steep climb up to the town where it was about a kilometre from the Cathedral. Then it was that same distance back to catch the bus again. He could organise a car to take us instead. That would be better.

I had already asked back at the Royal Palace how much a taxi ride was and couldn't believe the exorbitant price they told us. We agreed on a much lower price with the man and I double checked the price included my scooter as well as the three of us. This seemed the best option. Time was limited, we were not sure about the bus anyway and we went with the flow of where we were. He signalled someone to pick us up.

A keen young man drove over in his brightly coloured tiny car. We all stuffed in and he took off. He drove fast, but we could see out enough to take in the view as we went up the mountain. The Tyrrhenian Sea was a wonderful blue extending out from the sprawling city stretching along the coastline below.

On the way I checked if the price included being picked up after a few hours. No, it was for one way.

'Send a message to my phone on WhatsApp and I will come and get you,' he said as he wrote his number while still driving.

We could see the final climb was long and difficult on narrow one-way streets with no footpaths and only cars speeding up and down.

Inside the cathedral at Monreale it was crowded but enough room for everyone to move about, most with their mouths open in wonder and eyes looking everywhere. The enormous building has mosaics lining everything inside with so many figures and so much gold. Apparently, tens of thousands of kilograms of pure gold were used to create these 6,000 square metres of mosaics in the 12th-century.

I have been to a few churches in the world where the artwork–paintings, sculptures, carvings and the like have been outstanding. But the Byzantine mosaics here were the best artwork I'd ever seen.

Looking up at the ceilings, arches and walls, the characters of the bible tell their stories as expressive figures in mosaics on a gold background. One woman visiting had binoculars to look at the work more closely. The most impressive figure is the face of Christ above and back from the altar. It is 13m wide and 7m high and is the figure seen on postcards – Gesù Cristo il Pantocratore, sec. X11.

Even the steps up to the altar had gold mosaics in their vertical rises in geometric designs. Other patterns of mosaics lower on the walls are more familiar Islamic art.

After our visit we lined up at a taxi rank outside displaying a reasonable price back to the city. The queue grew, but no taxi came. Finally, a van arrived and told us the cost for a shared lift for a minimum of ten. There were twelve of us, plus my scooter, and it cost a fraction of the price we paid to get there.

Next morning queues were already outside the Palazzo dei Normanni (Norman Palace) or Royal Palace of Palermo, but waiting was easy looking up at the building. Its Arab-Norman-Byzantine style was something else unique. More square than other castles, with many levels and intricate stonework.

A guide approached us soon after entering and took us along an accessible route through the palace to the chapel. The route took us into secured areas with artwork, narrow passageways, decorative hallways, private lifts, rooms where the regional parliament met, and other areas not generally seen. While accessing one area we went onto a balcony overlooking a courtyard and found we were on a beautiful circular three-tiered white loggia with arches.

At another stage we exited a lift onto a brown and grey marble tiled floor with a set of steps to one side. The guide directed me forward before telling me to stop and wait. Then the floor rose below me with my scooter and me on it! A rectangular segment of tiled area, blending in with the rest of the floor, moved up. Once I was level with the floor above, a plate directly underneath the scooter moved forward over the first steps to meet the next floor.

On a lifter in a palace floor in Palermo

To my astonishment, I rode straight out.

We went past other rooms in the palace, with separate ticketed entry, on the way to the chapel. That whet our appetites with glimpses of gold, gems and mosaics on walls and ceilings.

A glimpse inside a room at the Palazzo Normanni

It wasn't easy on my scooter, shuffling along inside the smaller Pallatine chapel amongst the tightly packed crowd. While we were all inching along, thankfully most of the sights were found looking upwards to the ceiling, the dome or walls high up. That is where the oldest mosaics dating back to the 12th Century again are. Gold, sparkling gold. Much like the cathedral the day before - beauty beyond description.

The chapel is much smaller than the cathedral in Monreale, and the mosaics seemed brighter. The small pieces of materials – stone, glass (stained, enamelled) or ceramic – in different colours were intricately arranged. It was the gold-plated pieces that stood out again-shimmering, each one different, sparkling and combining to form images.

The sight could be mistaken for several paintings, but they are not, and paintings don't have luminescence like these.

The interior was completely covered in encrusted golden mosaics. No one photo could really show what it was like, so I took a video instead. I could see why the chapel is called Sicily's greatest work of Arab-Norman art.

I was surprised at how wonderful those two places in Palermo were. When I returned friends asked what the places were like and I had trouble telling them because the places defied adequate description. You just have to see them for yourself.

From Palermo we caught the train to Syracuse. I thought I knew about the train system in Sicily from reading, downloading maps and asking a few questions. Most people told me to catch a bus, not a train, but I thought the train route would be more scenic, especially the fast one travelling along the northern coastline then down the east coast to Syracuse. When we bought tickets for the train the day before at Palermo Centrale, I thought we were purchasing tickets for that route. Communicating was difficult and when the ticket officer told us the departure times and the time of four and a half hours with one change of train in Catania, that sounded good.

We saw the northern coastline for a short while before it never reappeared. The train went south-east through the middle of Sicily. The surprise ended up being a good one because that was the only time, we saw the rural countryside. Open rocky bare spaces and agricultural farming lands were interspersed between at least two mountaintop towns. The buildings were only at the top of the mountains and I had not seen towns like that before.

One plain we went across must have been very arable as every part of it was cultivated with olives, fruit trees and pomegranates. Lemon and olive groves popped up again between grasslands under bridges between mountains and raised motorways, the closer we got to Catania. I suddenly realised where we were when an immense mountain appeared covered in cloud.

'Look that must be Mt Etna over there on the left. We must be somewhere south of it.' I said, pointing to a spot on a very rough map.

We changed trains in Catania and got out of our nice comfortable clean Trenitalia train with easy access for my scooter. Our next train was supposed to be on the other side of the same platform. And there was a train waiting. But it only had two carriages with graffiti painted all over it, including the windows. Some graffiti looked a bit arty and professional, but not on the windows, obliterated with spray. I thought it was waiting to go off for repairs.

But it was the correct train, and we noted the very high steps to get into the carriage. We got the scooter up with help from a man from Portugal.

On the train, about halfway between Catania and Syracuse, the air outside changed. Pale grey smoke filled the air surrounding us, coming from not just one factory chimney stack but hundreds! Kilometre after kilometre we moved past smelly petrochemical plants on the edge of the coast where ships were moored. It was a terrible sight.

At one point, the train went over a waterway with green slimy water in a small lake on one side. The ground and air looked very polluted. It was an enormous area and I read later it is the largest refinery area in Europe with numerous oil and energy production companies operating. There was a train station amidst it all too, with rows of houses in a township–how did they breathe?

Our renovated apartment in an old building in Syracuse was large, with an outdoor terrace looking out over the town, to the island of Ortigia (or Ortygia) and the sea on either side. I had seen the floor plan and was impressed with the two bathrooms with showers and a toilet in each. But I was most surprised to find one was in a cupboard at the end of a hallway. The toilet had a hand pump, and the shower was a plastic pod sitting beside it. There was no fresh air and it smelt. We left the door closed and used the other one.

We spent our first days visiting the ancient island of Ortygia. We could walk there in under 10 minutes. Two small bridges over a narrow waterway separated the island from the mainland. A statue of Archimedes welcomed us just past the bridge, celebrating his birth in 288 BC. A Greek mathematician and scientist born in Syracuse when it was part of Greece, not Italy.

Off the touristed main strips, the many back streets of the town were a joy to walk through. Narrow passageways and alleys were enclosed by two and three storey lightly coloured stone houses. A few had clothes hanging out neatly, drying on balconies. Some streets had shops and restaurants at ground level, with small trees and plants growing along edges or in courtyards. It was perfect for walking-cool in the hot day, so much to see.

Historic buildings popped up here and there – an abbey, a small church, a plaza, a statue and a grand basilica. Ortygia is large enough to get lost in, but small enough to be for only a little while. Sometimes the simplest domestic sights were the best.

Along one narrow laneway, three tables sat outside a small restaurant where the sound of something cooking gently and the smell of fennel caught our attention. It looked like just the kind of genuine local family restaurant we had been looking for. From the Primi Piatti section of the menu, I chose Pasta con le sarde e salsa al finocchietto (Pasta with sardinian and fennel sauce). It was delicious.

Most of the passageways had smooth ground for my scooter. There were only a few where the stone was raised and cobbly. On the backstreets we were often the only people there. We made sure we walked over the whole island from the Castle at the southern tip, to the Fort on the Ionian Sea east side and to the beach promenade on the Port Grande west side. Returning to the bridge after a gelato along the way.

After a few days in Syracuse, we realised we had to visit the Parco Archeologico della Neapolis or Archeological Park in the opposite direction to Ortygia. It was supposed to be an important site because of some ruins. What an understatement! The size and intact state of the largest, perfectly preserved Greek amphitheatre that I'd ever seen just hit me. Obviously, I had done little reading or research before we left. It is a classical masterpiece.

At the top of the amphitheatre, there were recesses or holes in the rocks from prehistoric burial spaces. Another jaw dropper!

The amphitheatre was in the open air and I could go around on my scooter at the base, up on one level and also around at the top to look at the Neapolis.

On my scooter at the Teatro Greco, Syracuse

Signs around explained the 5th-century-BC Teatro Greco was a place for plays, orations and music and could hold 16,000 people. I learned Greek amphitheatres are different to Roman ones. And there was one of those in the park, too. The nearby Roman Amphitheatre or Anfiteatro Romano, built later in the 2nd -century AD, was where gladiatorial contests, mock battles or exotic animal hunts took place. Much was left to the imagination as the crumpled left-over Roman ruins are overrun with weeds and grasses.

Our route to and from the train station in Syracuse was always different, never finding the best accessible way. There were always roads to cross without crossings, roadworks, footpaths with no ramps and sometimes no footpaths at all. Being on my scooter was difficult.

Some trains were nicer than others. The small old one covered in graffiti chugged along noisily. We had been on it a few times and were still working out a technique to load the scooter. The lifter used for persons with a disability was sitting in a room at the station behind glass, looking lovely. But it was never brought out, and when we asked for it, they said it was broken. Train guards and attendants never offered to help. We tried to avoid that train.

I noted that a high-speed train going to Rome left from Catania. I hoped the access would be better and there might be a chance of getting disabled assistance. I sent an email to the advertised disability help site a few days before trying to get to Catania. They replied, *thank you... but it is not possible.*

We still wanted to go to Catania, and I wanted to get the high-speed train. On the day, after we had negotiated our way to the station, we lined up at the ticket office. We had allowed plenty of time and were pleased when we saw a nice train waiting.

Inside, the Syracuse train station was abuzz, and people were not moving out of there fast. Some queued at the two automatic ticket machines and didn't move because there were no tickets coming out. The machines seemed to be broken. We stuck with the queue lining up for the man behind the glass window under the Ticket Office sign with another handmade sign underneath – *No tourist information given here.*

More people came into the area with everyone nervously talking, and it was almost time for the train to leave. I was sitting on my scooter and as soon as I moved to the window to buy tickets, the man closed the small gap in the window and put up another sign. *Ticket Office Closed.* I tried to tell the man that we really needed to get some tickets. There were other people waiting behind me too.

But he said, 'Machine not working, computer problem'. He then left and went outside to have a cigarette. And presumably a break.

What could we do but just get on the train? We had already caught several trains, validated the tickets on the platform, and no-one had ever checked.

It was a nice train, comfortable upholstery, unlike the old, marked vinyl on the small train. Clean passageways, clean windows, easy to just ride my scooter in and it felt like a proper train.

Any train guards we'd seen before sat up front with the engine driver for the whole trip, or if off the train just chatted with their fellow workers.

That was until that trip. We were the only people in the carriage until a smartly dressed train guard in a blue suit with matching cap came through and asked for our tickets. When we explained what happened, the young man said there was a fine of €50 per person for not having a ticket. We kept telling him we really tried but couldn't buy a ticket. Somehow, he decided to let us off.

'This time', he said. A nice surprise.

I found Catania to be a decrepit place. Centuries-old buildings with intricate architecture had been left uncared for, parts rusting, parts falling down, with weeds and mould growing over them. It wasn't just one or two buildings but streets of them side by side. It was not a pleasant walk in the old part of the city.

The place brightened up when we found the open food market with a multitude of colourful umbrellas grouped together as a covering over the passageways. Looking up, it looked more like an Asian scene than an Italian one.

The train station at Catania was more substantial than the one at Syracuse. There were several platforms, and it looked like a major transport hub. Standing outside we could see Mt Etna, active, with smoke coming out the top.

Buying tickets was not a problem but getting to platform 4 was. We found an underpass with many steps down. I waited on my scooter while Sue and Robin went to ask where the lift was or the accessible route. When they came back the story was that people just shrugged their shoulders.

Sue started to move the scooter down the steps, and I walked slowly with my sticks. A young woman offered to help, making things easier going down, but then we had the next set of steps to get up to the platform. Sue went one step at a time, pulling the scooter. At the top, the funny train with the graffiti was waiting with five train attendants standing chatting.

When the carriage doors opened, getting up the high steps onto the train was the same as before. We sent Robin ahead to save three seats. I pulled myself up and positioned myself to take the top end of the scooter and roll it in after Sue lifted the front. Several people came past us to get seats. We left the scooter, brake on, in the entry area of the carriage.

We had all had quite enough of those odd trains and vowed never to get another one.

Mt Etna held a fascination for all of us, and we wanted to get closer. The local tourist information in Ortygia suggested a trip via the towns of Nicolosi and Zafferana. Several buses went there but not directly from Syracuse and connection times did not flow easily.

Walking back home afterwards, we noticed the Italian travel agency we used for our Palermo accommodation. We booked a driver through them to take us (with my scooter) for a three to four-hour trip to the two towns and back to see Mt Etna.

Maria picked us up on a morning from our apartment. Our drive along the freeway went through new countryside with lemons growing in orchards everywhere.

Her English was not good, but enough for us to understand and chat. Mt Etna held a special place in Sicilian hearts, 'our mother', active for millions of years with all sorts of stories, legends and myths. Her rich fertile soils providing well.

After driving through Nicolosi, at the foot of Mt Etna, we were surprised to continue on a road up the southern side of the mountain. We were not sure how close we might get but did not expect to go up.

We drove past houses and land devastated from past eruptions, especially the one in 2001 lasting weeks, as we went higher and higher. Among the bushes, old black lava flows rolled down the side of the mountain like rivers. At a lookout, we stopped for photos and quickly put on our warm jackets in the cold. Maria used her phone to give us Googled English information and two bicycle riders came by and stopped too. We looked up at several peaks and areas on the summit where white and brown smoke were puffing out. We were getting excited.

Maria parked the car at the highest point on the road, Cantoniera d'Etna, where many cars were parked around a variety of tourist facilities.

I raised my eyebrows when I saw chair lifts with people aboard going up towards the smoking active volcano. Others were walking up steep extinct volcanic outlets with gravelly sides of reddish-brown and black slag. Patches of yellow and green foliage helped make that area look safer. Ashes, sand and fragments of lava lay on the ground as we walked and scootered around.

When we looked down the mountain back towards Catania, we found ourselves above the clouds. In a few areas, we could see the city and sea where the sun streamed through a break. A helicopter landing pad was perched on the edge and someone walked out to look down.

Helicopter pad at Mt Etna

Before returning to the car we stopped at a food van and tasted delicious artisan spreads made from pistachios grown on trees in nearby Bronte on the western slopes.

We left Mt Etna on the eastern side, going down past more old lava flows and destroyed buildings. Forests of chestnut, birch, beech and oak popped up on our twisting and turning descent. Lower down on more fertile soils we saw vineyards, olive groves and orchards. We had already bought some local wine called Etna Bianco and Etna Rosso, enjoying their complex mineral taste.

Leaving the village of Zafferana, going around and past the same place many times, we seemed lost. Maria pulled over a few times and spoke on the phone. We stopped shortly afterwards outside a garden area, not sure what we were doing.

Without explanation, Maria parked the car and told us to have a look around. We all walked around the garden and next thing we are seated inside a family restaurant and having lunch. We were hungry but thought we would be back in Syracuse in time. By then our three hours were up, and there was still more than an hour's drive to get back. Not knowing what to do, we all sat down, and Maria joined us.

She looked at the menus and selected items, pointing out some to us and then ordering. Surprised but not objecting, we went with the flow and ended up with a typical regional Sicilian meal of several courses. We thought we had finished when another course arrived! The portions were enormous. We met the family and tried to chat, but there were really just gestures and sounds being exchanged. We were the only people in the restaurant; we had photos taken of the four of us at the table and all enjoyed ourselves.

At the end we went to pay but Maria said no. She explained the meal was included in our trip and the owner had not charged her. She said the owner was a friend of her brother's and that was who she was ringing before to find out where the place was. She wanted to make sure she gave us a good time.

We all enjoyed each other's company and the day. To finish off, Maria jumped out on the way back and bought some almond and pistachio biscotti as a farewell gift. Our day out to Mt Etna towards the end of our trip turned out to be one of the best.

Other days included going up steep roads into the baroque town of Noto where without footpaths my mobility scooter decided it needed to be a motor scooter on the road; visiting a beach in Fontaine Bianchi, surprised when asked to pay; and being amongst pilgrims to the landmark modern Basilica, with the incredible name, Santuario Madonna delle Lacrime (the shrine to Our Lady of Tears).

During our stay locals talked of deformed babies in the town of the petrochemical plant, Russian oligarchs making money then buying up old properties and the benefits of eating cannelloni. Our stay in that part of Sicily was most memorable.

Buses went regularly from Syracuse to Catania Airport, and the bus stop was just around the corner. I had a timetable from one of the nurses at the day clinic in Melbourne. Katrina picked one up for me during her family holiday a few months before. She gave me a map of Syracuse and the bus timetable.

'I would get a taxi if I were you,' she said after giving me the timetable. Katrina explained the bus they caught broke down on the way to the airport and everyone had to get out with their luggage on the expressway and wait for a long time for another bus. Everyone was worried they might miss their plane. Apparently, it wasn't unusual. We enquired about the bus, but they told us wheelchairs or scooters were not allowed. That sealed it. I booked a taxi transfer to the airport.

The weather had been perfectly warm and dry during our stay with temperatures in the mid 20°Cs but on the last day rain bucketed down. We had to vacate our apartment in the morning and our flights were not leaving Catania until much later. We sat in the shelter of a variety of cafes for hours, waiting for the time to pass. After a wonderful lunch of Sicilian pizza, the taxi picked us up.

It was hard to see anything outside as we drove in the heavy rain. It continued for the whole hour to get to the airport.

Inside the terminal it was eerily quiet. Before long, it was obvious something was not right. People were gathering in small groups and talking seriously, others were queueing in front of airline desks with rough hand-written signs above, saying *Information Here.*

There was a transport-workers' strike across all of Italy. All flights leaving Fontanarossa Airport Catania had been cancelled for several hours. Nothing was flying again until the evening, with flights starting just before Sue's and my flight. Robin was not going on the earlier EasyJet flight to London.

The only help at information was to go online and see if your airline would substitute another flight or just book another one. Regardless, the first flight out of Catania going to London was next Tuesday, and this was Friday.

A man nearby also going to London suggested Robin book a hotel near the airport where he was staying with a group so they might meet up for a drink at the bar to pass the time. He had already booked a Tuesday flight and said there were not many seats left.

After our day trip to Catania, there was no way Robin wanted to stay in a hotel anywhere near there.

Sue and I were flying to Zurich to catch a flight home the next day. Before the flight we were meeting up with Thilli and Anni, who were coming down from Germany by train to meet us for lunch. We thought we were lucky our flight from Catania still looked good to go.

There was no internet access where we were at the airport and no-where for Sue and Robin to sit. I had my scooter. Some buckets were out on the floor with water coming in here and there on the ground floor.

McDonalds was up on the first floor and could usually be relied upon for Wi-Fi. The place was packed when we entered. Everyone who had arrived downstairs seemed to be now up in McDonalds. It was hard to find a place to sit, especially with everyone's luggage beside them. We joined groups on two tables where we were at one end and could link across. Sue and I were not leaving for hours and came early with Robin to keep her company. I conjured up a plan.

'Why not come to Zurich with us?' I suggested. 'There might be spare seats on our flight. You could stay at our hotel and book a flight from Zurich to London tomorrow. There should be plenty from there.'

After much discussion, that was the plan. I logged on to Swiss Air and their Edelweiss Air flights from Catania to Zurich. I was able to do an Economy class booking but as it was being confirmed my internet access cut out and I had to start all over again. I tried again, and again but every time the Wi-Fi cut out. It was hard to be fast on my iPhone, and time allowed on the internet was limited. I must have asked Robin the name and number on her credit card so many times that I could see faith in what I was doing was wavering.

I needed coffee. Black and strong and got it. With sheer determination and grit, I pressed on to get this booking done! I must have become quicker because confirmation eventually came through. But it was only to say they were unable to make a booking at this stage.

'What about Business Class?' I enquired out loud. Robin held her breath and said nothing. Sue didn't say anything either. Back I went onto the website. I was able to book a Business Class seat and waited and 'prayed' with clenched hands for the confirmation.

'Yes, got it. Done. Rob, you are coming to Zurich with us!'

'Great, but how do I get to London?'

'Let's book that now too?'

'Okay. I like British Airways. I've always found them good.'

It was easy booking a flight from Zurich to London and I didn't have to ask Robin for her details over and over again, just the once.

'Now somewhere to stay the night.'

I stopped and took a breather. The crowd in McDonalds had not decreased, people were still everywhere. Burgers were still being cooked and fries were on every table. We had packed a sandwich for ourselves and eaten it, so we were okay.

'Switzerland is expensive, isn't it?' asked Robin.

'Yes, it is. But they might be able to fit another bed in the room.'

The hotel replied to my email quickly and said there was plenty of room and the cost was a small additional fee. Booked.

All we had to do then was cross our fingers and hope we would all get out of there together that night.

My scooter was the next thing to worry about. It had not been in this airport before. There always seemed to be some sort of problem. But we were on our way home and as long as we got to Zurich, we could make do with whatever happened.

Nothing bad happened. Robin had a lovely time in Business Class while we waved from Economy. There was plenty of room in the hotel for all of us, and Robin flew out the next morning. There were no surprises after we left Sicily, and too many to count while we were there.

We met Thilli and Anni for lunch and walked in the parklands along the shores of Lake Zurich. All four of us enjoyed walking together, chatting, especially in gardens and noticing what is flowering.

The trees revealed their autumn colours in a cold late October, and I looked forward to returning to the warmth of Melbourne and our spring flowers.

I eagerly await seeing all overseas friends again, somewhere soon, on another trip with more surprises, adventures, parks and gardens. And more walking and wheeling.

In closing

A Woman Who Goes Out Walking/
A Local Travel Triptych
(2020) Section 2

The prolific garden of trees and flowers spills over from the house on the corner to the road. The sun is always shining on some part. The woman who goes out walking often finished her walk going past the house with verges facing north and west, with a flow over jungle area facing north-east.

The owner gardening lover is often out there when the woman goes past and always says hello using her name. The woman greets her back and sometimes she stops.

The woman loves walking past the yellow hibiscus flowers and admiring their colours – the stamen with yellow dots and red dots arising at the end and the gorgeous yellow colour of the petals coming out of a red centre with orange-yellow rays that look like the sun. The woman walking noticed when the edges of the yellow petals were changing colour to a pinkie shade with age and told the gardener how wonderful they were.

The younger gardener agreed and called them 'beauties', saying how much she enjoyed watching them grow ever since she planted them, and told the woman it is a 'Tequila Sunrise' hibiscus.

The woman smiled and told the gardener there was always something wonderful happening in her garden. Appreciating the compliment, the gardener quickly pointed out how much she enjoyed being out there.

Later in 2020, on some other days the woman was seen in suburbs nearby, when it was allowed. Sometimes she was standing at the side of a car while someone was getting her walker out. And a few times she was seen on the walking track around Albert Park Lake. The woman was travelling locally as well as in the neighbourhood.

There is a woman who goes out walking along the beachfront. The sand is too soft for her walker but the concrete walkway beside it, nicely separated from the bike trail with palm trees, native grasses and seats, is perfect. She is there at least once a week, arriving out of the neighbourhood or from the pier.

A few years ago, when the woman was on the way to the beach, some Asian tourists in tight jeans and sunhats stopped her at the corner where the lines of gum trees and palm trees meet.

'We are looking for the Pink Lake. Do you know which way?' they asked, holding small books opened at a page.

'It's about two kilometres that way,' the woman said, pointing west. 'Over there in a park under the Westgate Bridge,' she added, hoping they understood as they walked off.

The woman thought to herself she had never been to the Pink Lake and had just met visitors from overseas wanting to see it. She must have a look one day.

She always thinks when she is out walking and often talks to herself, but never out loud.

Bright yellow bollards with a red and white band signal her way to the beach through the neighbourhood bush reserve.

She walks easily on the new bitumen path running off the footpath in a gap between banksia and casuarina trees. As she moves forward the woman can feel the soft but firm bounciness in the path that seems to have been made especially for wheels and walking. The woman appreciates this path as it is much better than the old pebbly gravel track and she can look around more easily. It is quieter too.

Each time, she looks up at the banksia trees to find the yellow cones and see what stage they are at. Flowering across all seasons, she is always likely to find some. The woman has loved discovering many other colourful banksias in her Australian travels.

The five tall, automated stacking towers at the nearby dock become more obvious further along the path. They look like giraffes, as the person on Instagram commented. She has noted a lot more noise coming from there since the pandemic started and would like to know why.

The woman walks on through mown green lawn on either side, good for picnics or just lolling about, and sees the water of Port Phillip Bay ahead. She stops briefly where all paths meet around a triangle of saltbush with old pier timbers at the base and *1839 LIARDET'S JETTY* neatly chiselled. The salt bush is growing over most of the lettering and the woman wonders if she should bring along secateurs to trim it.

The bike trail has cyclists whizzing past, and the woman looks left and right, before walking over Look, Bike warning signs to get to the beach path.

'The seaside has a special flair about it,' one of the woman's German friends said one time when they were walking along the Baltic Sea on a holiday. The woman out walking agreed and loves her beach walks.

With more time on her hands during the pandemic, she has been out walking more often and trying to go further, bit by bit. The woman turns right, taking the longer route beside Sandridge Beach where dogs are allowed off leash in winter. They love to play and leave their paw prints in the orderly pattern of tyre tracks left in the sand after the beach sweeper.

The woman walks towards the modern glass building of Life Saving Victoria at the far end of the beach. She might see a ship in dock in the distance behind the building, but it still doesn't obscure the tall chimney stack on the other side of the Yarra River.

She walks under bowing night lights rising out of native grass running down the middle in a line between walking path and bike trail. Facing away from each other, the taller one towers over her as she walks, while the shorter one bends over the bike trail.

Before the pandemic really started, a woman in tasteful casual dress with a sheltie met her on the beachfront. They appeared to know each other, judging by the cheerful greeting and instant patting and talking with the dog.

'When's your next trip? Anything booked?' the other woman asked as the dog lay down, knowing it would be more than a quick hello.

The woman out walking pushed her sun hat back and sat on her walker replying, 'We were so lucky. For the first time, we had nothing booked. I think we will be seeing more of Australia for a while. Go over to Western Australia and drive up north from Perth. We haven't seen the section between Perth and Coral Bay. I thought we'd go in wildflower season later in the year.'

'Funny, I've booked a trip to see the wildflowers in Western Australia too. To do some drawing.' They talk about travel and the plays they'd booked, before the woman with the sheltie asked, 'Speaking about trips, where were you this time last year?'

'Alaska. On a cruise from Japan that went up across the Aleutian Islands to the Alaskan coast. The wild nature there was wonderful. But to be honest, I am really enjoying being at home now, walking every day, exploring and looking more closely at things around here – in the neighbourhood. I've been amazed at some of the things I've seen.'

Later in the pandemic, when they met again, the woman with the sheltie was quick to say, 'Looks like we won't be going to Western Australia. Or anywhere soon with all borders closed to us Victorians. The coronavirus numbers in Melbourne are terrible.'

'Yes, we'll have to rethink going anywhere this year. But I am still enjoying my walking. We have been driving to Albert Park, Middle Park and South Melbourne and going for walks around there too. We have found all sorts of new places. We even went down to see the Pink Lake the other day in Westgate Park.'

'I haven't been to the Pink Lake yet. We must go,' said the woman, looking lovingly at her dog.

They talked a bit more, keeping their social distance, and walked off in opposite directions.

The woman who goes out walking has a passion for travelling. She tries to go overseas once or twice a year and three times to Queensland. It is never for long, about four weeks, to fit in with her scheduled hospital visits. But she didn't need to consider that for the moment because she wasn't travelling anywhere outside Melbourne.

The woman walks past warning signs about currents, drops and submerged objects, each with a suitable scary symbol. During the COVID-19 pandemic there was another sign attached lower down the post warning people not to gather on the beach or sunbake and keep 1.5m apart.

She sometimes sits on the bench seats with the sun on her back and puts her legs up on her walker. The woman enjoys looking at the beach and everything around her, listening to bird calls from the bush behind her.

Up ahead children are laughing and calling out in the playground, and she recalls days in summer when Muslim families often gathered nearby. All ages enjoying being there together, women wearing hijabs and men with beards.

The woman walks on a bit more, but not much further because she has to get back. She adds that into her calculations because she can only walk for so far before her legs start to become paralysed. The woman has learnt the time and distance it takes but has been trying to push through and do more.

She used to be worried about going over six hundred metres. At the end of that time, she wasn't able to move one leg and found that frightening. What if she became stuck somewhere and couldn't get back home?

The woman checks and it is time to turn around at her latest marker, where *TURPENTINE Syncarpia glomulifera* is written on a piece of old timber at the edge of the path. The woman has already Googled that and knows it is a timber resistant to marine borers and termites used in wharf construction and thinks the wood was probably from one of the many old piers.

If she had her scooter, she could go all the way around to the Webb Point Observation Deck, past the containers on Webb Dock. But she was out there walking for the joy it brings in itself from moving and exercising, as well as doing local travel.

A few months after the pandemic started, a tall, fast walking, fit looking woman approached her near the turpentine timber saying, 'You've done well to get here.'

They both stopped and turned off the tracking apps on their phones.

'Yes, I'm walking much further. I suppose that's one positive thing from this pandemic.'

'Look where I went today,' said the fast walking woman showing the route on her phone.

'Six kilometres, that's good. I got to nearly two kilometres the other day. And, I've seen these amazing flowers earlier, see,' the woman out walking said as she showed the other woman the photo on her phone. 'I'll show you my route later.'

They both walked off on their own, one now two and half, (was three) times faster than the other.

Everyone out walking along the beach path is usually talking to the person beside them or on the phone. The seaside flair lends itself to socialising. But later in the pandemic people were not close enough to talk, and they were all wearing masks.

The woman walks back looking out on the bay and can see a container ship leaving, heading for the channel markers, with so many containers piled on each other she wonders why they don't all fall off with the slightest rolling wave.

When she arrives where the paths meet again, she walks straight ahead, letting the new bitumen path flow back to the road. The bike trail and walking path come together for a short distance before things really change. Waterfront beach houses and apartments spring up opposite the beach.

The night lights along the paths become colonial style with a goose neck shaped turn at the top over a short light shade. Tufts of native grass and seats sit below tall palm trees. She goes along New Beach towards Princes Pier. The beach called 'New' because it is new, created during the residential development.

In summer, motor cruisers drop anchor near the shore for a picnic. Seagulls squawking again. Then ahead, the true extent of the forest of piles on Princes Pier becomes more obvious.

In summer, the woman welcomes the arrival of shade under the palm trees. When she gets hot, she can't move her body as well and must cool down. It's a pleasant spot to rest with bay breezes and the sound of waves gently rolling in.

Once when she was sitting and checked her Email, she noticed one from her virtual physical therapy specialist in the U.S. Someone asked if they could regain muscle strength in their weaker leg? Yes, was the answer with neuroplasticity, explaining research proves through repeated exercise your brain works on finding a neural connection between your brain and the muscle. The woman is pleased she started the program of specific exercises, especially the ones to improve her balance and upper body strength. She had already experienced the mental benefits from brain stimulation, happening because of neuroplasticity, after actively looking at things and being open to her surroundings. She hoped her walking might benefit too.

Somewhere along the New Beach walk, the levels change, and the bike trail is higher. The woman is grateful for the ramp at the end, taking her up onto the pier where her beach walk ends.

Going home one day, she saw a woman in a driveway beside a campervan and said, 'Lovely sunny day. Nice Trakker van.'

'Yes, yes, it is,' the woman with the van replied and moved closer. They chatted about camping and travelling for a while before she added, 'I've seen you walking around for years now. Have you got a bad knee or hip?'

'No, I've got MS, multiple sclerosis,' the woman replied matter-of-factly.

'That's terrible. I wondered why you had a walker. I thought you didn't look old enough. That's awful.'

'No, it's fine. I'm doing well.'

'How long have you had it?'

'Probably twenty to thirty years. I didn't know I had it for ten years.'

'Really? You are doing well then. And the walker?'

'About twelve years. I think it's important to keep moving. Moving, moving.'

'Yes, I suppose it is. Nice talking with you.'

'Thanks,' said the woman who walked on thinking about the conversation. People react in different ways when they see someone using a walker.

When the woman gets back home each day, she looks at the tracking app on her phone and sees the distance, duration and pace of her walk. All three have improved during the pandemic. She wasn't fast, but she had built up her walking pace to walk one kilometre in twenty-three minutes, bettering her old benchmark of six hundred metres. The woman knew she was slower than most walkers, but it wasn't the speed that thrilled or interested her, it was the distance she was able to go and the length of time she was able to be outside walking. The woman had increased her distance to at least one and a half kilometres every day and was out for about forty-five minutes.

The woman who goes out walking loves the whole experience of walking–the way it makes her feel, the way it opens her eyes, the things she learns and what she sees or discovers. And she enjoys stopping too, standing or sitting on her walker and just observing something, sometimes absorbed in looking at, or smelling a flower. It's so satisfying she finds herself saying. No wonder she wants to go every day!

However, the woman who goes out walking (who is me) admits she also looks forward to travelling further away, again, soon.

Maureen T Corrigan

Walking and Wheeling Tales
© 2020 by Maureen T Corrigan

All Rights Reserved.

Shawline Publishing Group Pty Ltd
www.shawlinepublishing.com.au

SHAWLINE
PUBLISHING
GROUP

Lightning Source UK Ltd.
Milton Keynes UK
UKHW020002181220
375414UK00005B/34